Lecture Notes in Computer Science 13814

More information about this series at https://link.springer.com/bookseries/558

El Kindi Rezig · Vijay Gadepally ·
Timothy Mattson · Michael Stonebraker ·
Tim Kraska · Jun Kong ·
Gang Luo · Dejun Teng ·
Fusheng Wang (Eds.)

Heterogeneous Data Management, Polystores, and Analytics for Healthcare

VLDB Workshops, Poly 2022 and DMAH 2022
Virtual Event, September 9, 2022
Revised Selected Papers

Springer

Editors
El Kindi Rezig
Massachusetts Institute of Technology
Cambridge, MA, USA

Vijay Gadepally
Massachusetts Institute of Technology
Lexington, KY, USA

Timothy Mattson
Intel Corporation
Portland, OR, USA

Michael Stonebraker
Massachusetts Institute of Technology
Cambridge, MA, USA

Tim Kraska
Massachusetts Institute of Technology
Cambridge, MA, USA

Jun Kong
Georgia State University
Atlanta, GA, USA

Gang Luo
University of Washington
Seattle, WA, USA

Dejun Teng ⓘ
Shandong University
Qingdao, China

Fusheng Wang ⓘ
Stony Brook University
Stony Brook, NY, USA

ISSN 0302-9743   ISSN 1611-3349 (electronic)
Lecture Notes in Computer Science
ISBN 978-3-031-23904-5   ISBN 978-3-031-23905-2 (eBook)
https://doi.org/10.1007/978-3-031-23905-2

This Springer imprint is published by the registered company Springer Nature Switzerland AG
The registered company address is: Gewerbestrasse 11, 6330 Cham, Switzerland

Preface

In this volume we present the accepted contributions for the VLDB 2022 workshops entitled "Polystore systems for heterogeneous data in multiple databases with privacy and security assurances" (Poly 2022) and the "8th International Workshop on Data Management and Analytics for Medicine and Healthcare" (DMAH 2022). The workshops were held virtually in conjunction with the 48th International Conference on Very Large Data Bases during September 5–9, 2022.

The Poly workshop series focuses on the broader real-world polystore problem, which includes data management, data integration, data curation, privacy, and security. Enterprises are routinely divided into independent business units to support agile operations. However, this leads to "siloed" information systems which generate a host of problems, such as the following:

- Discovery of relevant data to a problem at hand. For example, Merck has 4000 (+/-) Oracle databases, a data lake, large numbers of files, and an interest in public data from the web. Finding relevant data in this sea of information is a challenge.
- Integrating the discovered data. Independently constructed schemas are never compatible.
- Cleaning the resulting data. A good figure of merit is that 10% of all data is missing or wrong.
- Ensuring efficient access to the resulting data. At scale operations must be performed "in situ", and a good polystore system is a requirement.

It is often said that data scientists spend 80% (or more) of their time on these tasks, and it is crucial to have better solutions. In addition, in 2018 the EU enacted the General Data Protection Regulation (GDPR) that forces enterprises to assuredly delete personal data on request. This "right to be forgotten" is one of several requirements of GDPR, and it is likely that GDPR-like requirements will spread to other locations, for example, California. In addition, privacy and security issues are increasingly an issue for large internet platforms. In enterprises, these issues will be front and center in the distributed information systems in place today. Lastly, enterprise access to data in practice will require queries constructed from a variety of programming models. A "one size fits all" model just won't work in these cases.

Poly 2022 received 3 submissions, which were reviewed in an single-blind process with each submission receiving at least 2 reviews. As a result, 3 papers were selected for presentation at the workshop and inclusion in this volume.

The DMAH workshop series focuses on the field cross-cutting information management and medical informatics. Healthcare enterprises are producing large amounts of data through electronic medical records, medical imaging, health insurance claims, surveillance, and other activities. Such data have high potential to transform current healthcare to improve healthcare quality and prevent diseases, and advance biomedical research. Medical informatics is an interdisciplinary field that studies and pursues the effective use of medical data, information, and knowledge for scientific inquiry, problem solving, and decision making, driven by efforts to improve human health and well-being.

The goal of the DMAH workshop is to bring people together to discuss innovative data management and analytics technologies highlighting end-to-end applications, systems, and methods to address problems in healthcare, public health, and everyday wellness, with clinical, physiological, imaging, behavioral, environmental, and omic - data, and data from social media and the Web. It provides a unique opportunity for interaction between information management researchers and biomedical researchers in this interdisciplinary field.

DMAH 2022 received 5 submissions, which were reviewed in a single blind process with each submission receiving at least 3 reviews. As a result, 3 papers were selected for presentation at the workshop and inclusion in this volume.

November 2022
El Kindi Rezig
Vijay Gadepally
Timothy Mattson
Michael Stonebraker
Tim Kraska
Jun Kong
Gang Luo
Dejun Teng
Fusheng Wang

Organization

POLY 2022

Workshop Chairs

El Kindi Rezig	MIT, USA
Vijay Gadepally	MIT, USA
Tim Kraska	MIT CSAIL, USA
Timothy Mattson	Intel Corporation, USA
Michael Stonebraker	MIT, USA

Program Committee Members

Vijay Gadepally	MIT, USA
El Kindi Rezig	MIT, USA
Danny Weitzner	MIT, USA
Michael Gubanov	FSU, USA
Edmon Begoli	ORNL, USA
Dimitris Kolovos	University of York, UK
Amarnath Gupta	UCSD, USA
Ratnesh Sahay	AstraZeneca, UK
Rada Chirkova	NCSU, USA
Sam Madden	MIT, USA
Tim Kraska	MIT, USA
Pedro Pedreira	Facebook Inc., USA
Timothy Mattson	Intel Corporation, USA
Michael Stonebraker	MIT, USA
Mourad Ouzzani	Qatar Computing Research Institute, Qatar
Makoto Onizuka	University of Osaka, Japan
Ahmed Abdelhamid	Purdue University, USA
Ismail Oukid	Snowflake, USA

DMAH 2022

Workshop Chairs

Jun Kong	Georgia State University, USA
Gang Luo	University of Washington, USA
Dejun Teng	Shandong University, China
Fusheng Wang	Stony Brook University, USA

Program Committee Members

Ablimit Aji	Kouper Health, USA
Luca Bonomi	Vanderbilt University, USA
Yang Cao	Kyoto University, Japan
Jerome Carter	Informatics Squared, Inc., USA
Peter Elkin	University at Buffalo, USA
Vagelis Hristidis	University of California, Riverside, USA
Tahsin Kurc	Stony Brook University, USA
Ying Wang	Macquarie University, Australia
Ye Ye	University of Pittsburgh, USA
Xiaxia Yu	Shenzhen University, China
Xiaoyi Zhang	University of Washington, USA

Invited Talk

Health Informatics in the Age of AI

Shlomo Berkovsky

Australian Institute of Health Innovation, Center for Health Informatics,
Macquarie University, Sydney, Australia
shlomo.berkovsky@mq.edu.au

Abstract. This talk will overview the breadth of research carried out by the Centre for Health Informatics at the Australian Institute of Health Innovation. We will initially discuss the 3 streams of ongoing work – Precision Health, Human-Technology Interaction, and Physiological Clinical Predictors – and then delve into the upcoming promising directions inspired by the recent developments in sensing technologies, cloud computing, and machine learning.

Spatial Data Management for Medicine and Healthcare

Dejun Teng

School of Computer Science and Technology, Shandong University, Qingdao, China
teng@sdu.edu.cn

Abstract. The development of spatially enabled applications such as the Internet of Things and ubiquitous positioning services leads to strong demands for efficient spatial data processing in both 2D and 3D space. Meanwhile, large-scale spatial data has gained extensive attention in the medicine and healthcare domain with the development of contact tracing, medical imaging, human atlases, and digital pathology. While significant effort has been made on studying distributed spatial data processing, there exist major challenges to the efficient processing of complex spatial objects, such as complex polygons with many edges, and 3D polyhedrons with many faces, with traditional spatial models and Filter and Refine Strategy. For instance, pathologists want to conduct queries over spatial data extracted from 2D or 3D medical images for better diagnosing the development of diseases. In the contact tracing scenario, it is critical to retrieve the contacted individuals from billions of trajectories in real-time. In this talk, I will introduce typical researches we have conducted for improving the efficiency of managing the spatial data in medicine and healthcare domains.

Contents

POLY 2022

Ad-hoc Searches on Image Databases

Oscar Moll[1]([✉]), Sam Madden[1], and Vijay Gadepally[2]

[1] MIT CSAIL, Cambridge, MA, USA
orm@csail.mit.edu
[2] MIT Lincoln Laboratory, Lexington, MA, USA

Abstract. Searching for ad-hoc objects in image and video datasets can be expensive and time consuming. As image data is more common, we increasingly need systems to help us query it. In this talk, we describe related work and then explore two approaches: ExSample [14] and See-Saw [15] which target different scenarios of image and video search.

Keywords: Ad-hoc image search · Image search systems · Interactive image search

1 Introduction

Searching for objects in image and video datasets can be expensive and time consuming, but such searches are important building blocks in larger workflows. For instance, a company collecting self-driving car video data may want to develop detection for specific new types of objects, such as wheelchairs, as part of its development process. The first step in this task is to collect a few examples of wheelchairs from the unlabeled dataset in order to construct a basic training and test datasets. This search problem itself can be time consuming and expensive as databases can be too large for manual inspection, and models to recognize the objects can be either absent or expensive when run over a large amount of data.

2 Background and Related Work

Current work from the database community on querying video and image datasets varies along a several dimensions, four of them are: 1) The type of queries the system processes, such as a search for a type of object [12,15], or for a more complex event [1,6], or an analytic style query aggregating over the whole database [11]. 2) Assumptions about availability of pre-trained models, for example the existence of an object detector that works on the dataset. 3) The kind of indexing used by the system if any: indices built on object tracks or on feature vectors etc. 4) The optimization strategies used at query time, such as learning approximations for operators [11,13], sampling only subsets of the dataset, adapting resolutions, etc. We limit our discussion in this section to a

E. K. Rezig et al. (Eds.): DMAH 2022/Poly 2022, LNCS 13814, pp. 3–9, 2022.
https://doi.org/10.1007/978-3-031-23905-2_1

data warehouse setting where data has been collected, as opposed to work on a streaming setting with standing queries.

Different systems make different assumptions about what pre-trained models are available to answer queries. By models we mostly mean deep neural network models such as ResNet pretrained on ImageNet, FasterRCNN and CLIP, because they are the state of the art for most vision tasks at the moment. Absent any indexing, a naive approach to select frames satisfying a predicate (specified as a model, think of an object detector such as Faster-RCNN) is to scan the dataset with the model returning the frames where the object detector finds a specific object. The challenge with this approach is the high computational cost and the time it takes to process a large video database repeatedly with these models for different queries. Hence, many systems aim to lower this cost by approximating the operations, as in [13], or both.

Because image and video data can grow large in size quickly even if the data is only collected from a few cameras, and because scanning implicitly also involves computationally demanding compression decoding, repeatedly scanning images or video remains expensive even if the downstream operations are made approximate and cheap. In a data warehouse setting where data has accumulated over time, which is where we focus on in this talk, sub-linear times for executing queries, or at least some cheaper alternative to scanning video or images, are more desirable than paying a large linear overhead every time. This observation motivates the research for re-usable indices that we can compute once and re-use more cheaply, though the kinds of indices vary. Broadly speaking, indices split into track-based [1,2,6] and embedding based indices [10]. A track-based index is based on the observation that several types of queries on video can be reduced to running an object detector to find objects, tracking these over time, and then using these 'tracks' (bounding boxes over time) as a light-weight representation on which we can express more complex queries. For example a complex action of a person in a wheelchair crossing a street can be approximated by selecting wheelchair tracks and filtering those where the bounding box moves in the street crossing in the specified direction. The advantage of track indices is that if the relevant types of attributes are pre-computed, then the queries can be executed instantaneously, making these systems interactive. Moreover, many more complex queries involving combinations of events and object types can be expressed on top of this representation, not limited to simple selections. One limitation of track based indices is that they limit queries to be ad-hoc combinations of indexed concepts, but if wheelchairs were not indexed ahead of time, it is not clear how to proceed in searching for them either on their own or as part of a larger query.

The need for indices that can work beyond fixed taxonomies of objects motivates the use of semantic vector embedding of images. Pre-trained models such as ResNet [9] or CLIP [16] are widely used as a starting point for transfer learning, and can also be used simply as feature extractors mapping images to vectors in a high-level semantic space. Vectors extracted this way can be helpful for tasks for which the models were not explicitly trained for, and datasets these models were not trained on, so it makes sense using them as a starting point for indexing [17]. Given these higher level representations, different processing strategies are possible. For example, Voodoo Indexing [10] leverages a vector index and exploits the cluster structure that many datasets show to more quickly find samples that satisfy an expensive black box predicate (for example an object detector), and many active learning approaches can be implemented on top of this representation [5].

Whether there are indices present or not, query execution and index construction optimization strategies include approximation and sampling. On the approximation side, relevant knobs include modifying input size resolution, complex model distillation onto more run-time efficient query-specialized models. The sampling side includes frame rates, and random sampling based on some type of score [2–4].

Much approximation or sampling work above assumes there exists an expensive black box model and leverages approximations, or indices in order to minimize use of the model. In a number of real-world situations there is no relevant detection model available, either because the query is not part of any existing detector, for example, many pre-trained models like FasterRCNN will have fixed categories at training time, based on the labels they were trained on, or because the available detectors demonstrate poor performance on the specific datasets. Searching for wheelchairs in this scenario could be modeled as a similarity search problem, using an example wheelchair found in the database in order to retrieve more examples. However, while embeddings can provide a starting point, human input is often needed to verify these results. In this case we also want to minimize the amount of human effort it takes to carry out a task, which is related to work on Active Learning [18] and especially Active Search [7]. Work such as SEALS [5], SeeSaw [15] focus on human in the loop approaches to guide the search, while relying on feature vector index to be able to adapt quickly to user input. In particular, SEALS [5] addresses the scalability limits of active learning based search approaches by focusing on a small subset of the dataset, while [15] aims to have users guide searches with cross-modal embeddings such as CLIP [16].

In this talk we focus on two systems mentioned before: ExSample, and See-Saw.

3 ExSample

ExSample's goal is to process object search queries when we have a black box detector model, and a warehouse of video data without indexing. In video datasets, randomly sampling frames to inspect with an object detector can be far more effective a search strategy than any scanning based strategy, as scanning is expensive and contiguous frames redundant for most uses. ExSample exploits the empirical insight that results are usually not uniformly spread over time or over different individual files in video datasets. For example, wheelchairs are more likely to be present in cities rather than highways and more likely to appear during the day than at night in the same way as pedestrians are. Therefore, one way to help find results while saving on processing is to sample frames non-uniformly across the dataset according to this skew. This basic skewed sampling idea however can lead to over sampling, as redundancy in objects is a problem in video: if we sample frames from the same area too much, the positive results are likely to be views of the same objects some time apart.

Because ExSample does not know ahead of time where the skew is, the first problem is to learn this skew as it runs. ExSample approaches this first challenge by splitting the dataset into logical chunks, for example 20-minute intervals if a video is long, or individual video clips if they are shorter than that, and sampling from them, much as a multi-armed bandit model where each arm corresponds to a chunk of the dataset and the reward for an arm draw is finding a positive result. If the distribution of results in the different chunks is skewed, as it is shown in Fig. 1, then there is potential for savings by allocating samples to the chunk with the largest number of results.

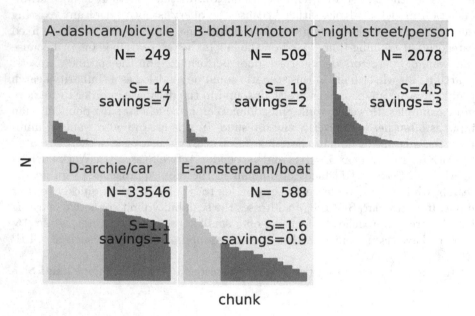

Fig. 1. Instance skew across chunks of datasets is evident. The larger the skew, the more ExSample can help savings

A naive bandit model approach in this setting would estimate the probability of finding a "positive" frame for each chunk, and over time allocate samples to the chunk with the largest hit-ratio, balancing between exploration and exploitation using techniques such as Thompson Sampling. This approach is too greedy, as the hit ratio is unable to distinguish two different wheelchairs appearing a few seconds apart from two frames showing the same wheelchair a few seconds apart.

Users always have the option to scan nearby frames if that would be useful to them, hence exploiting this type of low hanging fruit can be left to the user and is not the metric of interest.

ExSample instead aims to optimize finding distinct results. To enable this, ExSample requires the user to provide an additional black box (a 'comparator', distinct from the object detector) that decides if two results from the object detector are distinct (one way to implement this would be via some similarity score and a threshold). Instead of estimating the reward of a chunk based on a simple frame hit rate, one of ExSample's contributions is an estimate of the expected number of *new* results in a chunk in a future draw. This estimate is similar to and inspired by the Good-Turing [8] missing mass estimator, but ExSample's estimate is adapted to a setting where many or no results can appear in the same frame. One key feature of our estimate is that it does not make assumptions about how long a result appears on the screen (either on average or otherwise). Indeed, the time duration of single tracks of objects in video streams seem to follow a highly-variable distribution, so assuming a specific duration threshold would be misguided, and the longest instances would dominate results. The distribution information relevant for estimation is implicitly acquired from the comparator, and captured statistically as the number of results that have been seen exactly once. Finally, because we need to use our estimate in a bandit setting, we also develop an estimate of its error suitable for use with Thompson Sampling. By using this estimate, ExSample balances exploring chunks with uncertain results, allocating samples to chunks with more results, and gradually allocates samples away from even those chunks that initially yielded more results, as new results become harder to find.

ExSample offers a way to allocate samples to different parts of a dataset. One limitation of the approach is that the sampling allocation is adjusted only at a coarse (chunk) level, due to lack of fine-grained information about each frame. Within each chunk ExSample will draw a random sample. ExSample assumes there is a black-box model that captures what a result is. In the next section we explain SeeSaw, a system for image searches designed for a flipped scenario, one where there is no black box model, but there is an index with fine grained information.

4 SeeSaw

SeeSaw is designed for a scenario where we want to search for an ad-hoc concept in an image database. The goal is to enable the user to search for objects in the database and find some examples, even if these objects are rare and there is no object detector model available. In fact, SeeSaw is motivated by the need to help users develop a detector model or extend one, and this is the reason we are searching the database in the first place. For this scenario, the first goal is to find a few examples in order to build a training and test sets and SeeSaw aims to help users construct these.

To enable ad-hoc searches, SeeSaw makes use of visual-semantic embedding models such as CLIP [16]. The embedding model allows us to extract meaningful features from images which we can index and look up quickly, and also allows us to align these representations with text strings on a semantic level, so that searching for the string "wheelchair" is likely to help you find images with some content related to wheelchairs.

CLIP as a stand-alone solution for search on your own data falls short in multiple ways. One of them is highly variable accuracy for different queries. A search for wheelchairs on the BDD dataset [19] takes more than 100 images to find a handful of examples. As with wheelchairs, there is a long tail of queries hard to anticipate ahead of time for which a user may not be able to quickly find results [15]. One important insight for SeeSaw is that a small amount of user input at query time can go a long way in helping the user find useful results in practice, because errors are not random. Instead, different error types show up repeatedly. Exploiting this insight helps users find positive results faster if they provide input to the system.

User input to SeeSaw is in two forms: text strings describing the type of object of interest in natural language, as well as region-box feedback identifying useful results if any are shown. How this input is integrated into the decision of which images to show next is important, as user input can also worsen search results when compared to a non-interactive baseline. To incorporate feedback constructively, SeeSaw internally must balance the importance given to user feedback with the weight given to CLIP predictions.

References

1. Bastani, F., et al.: MIRIS: fast object track queries in video. In: Proceedings of the 2020 ACM SIGMOD International Conference on Management of Data, SIGMOD 2020, pp. 1907–1921. Association for Computing Machinery, New York (2020). https://doi.org/10.1145/3318464.3389692
2. Bastani, F., Madden, S.: OTIF: Efficient tracker pre-processing over large video datasets. https://doi.org/10.1145/3514221.3517835. https://favyen.com/otif.pdf
3. Chin, T.W., Ding,R., Marculescu,D.: Adascale: towards real-time video object detection using adaptive scaling (2019)
4. Chunduri, P., Bang, J., Lu, Y., Arulraj, J.: Zeus: Efficiently localizing actions in videos using reinforcement learning. In: Proceedings of the 2022 International Conference on Management of Data, SIGMOD 2022, pp. 545–558. Association for Computing Machinery, New York (2022). https://doi.org/10.1145/3514221.3526181
5. Coleman, C., et al.: Similarity search for efficient active learning and search of rare concepts (2020). http://arxiv.org/abs/2007.00077
6. Fu, D.Y., et al.: Rekall: specifying video events using compositions of spatiotemporal labels (2019). http://arxiv.org/abs/1910.02993
7. Garnett, R., Krishnamurthy, Y., Xiong, X., Schneider, J., Mann, R.: Bayesian optimal active search and surveying (2012). http://arxiv.org/abs/1206.6406
8. Good, I.J.: The population frequencies of species and the estimation of population parameters. Biometrika **40**(3/4), 237–264 (1953). https://doi.org/10.2307/2333344. http://www.jstor.org/stable/2333344
9. He, K., Zhang, X., Ren, S., Sun, J.: Deep residual learning for image recognition (2015). http://arxiv.org/abs/1512.03385

10. He, W., Anderson, M.R., Strome, M., Cafarella, M.: A method for optimizing opaque filter queries. In: Proceedings of the 2020 ACM SIGMOD International Conference on Management of Data, SIGMOD 2020, pp. 1257–1272. Association for Computing Machinery, New York (2020). https://doi.org/10.1145/3318464.3389766

11. Kang, D., Bailis, P., Zaharia, M.: BlazeIt: optimizing declarative aggregation and limit queries for neural network-based video analytics. Proc. VLDB Endow. **13**(4), 533–546 (2019). https://doi.org/10.14778/3372716.3372725

12. Kang, D., Emmons, J., Abuzaid, F., Bailis, P., Zaharia, M.: NoScope: optimizing neural network queries over video at scale. Proc. VLDB Endow. **10**(11), 1586–1597 (2017)

13. Lu, Y., Chowdhery, A., Kandula, S., Chaudhuri, S.: Accelerating machine learning inference with probabilistic predicates. In: Proceedings of the 2018 International Conference on Management of Data, SIGMOD 2018, pp. 1493–1508. Association for Computing Machinery, New York (2018)

14. Moll, O., Bastani, F., Madden, S., Stonebraker, M., Gadepally, V., Kraska, T.: ExSample: Efficient searches on video repositories through adaptive sampling (2020). http://arxiv.org/abs/2005.09141

15. Moll, O., Favela, M., Madden, S., Gadepally, V.: SeeSaw: interactive ad-hoc search over image databases (2022). http://arxiv.org/abs/2208.06497

16. Radford, A., et al.: Learning transferable visual models from natural language supervision (2021). http://arxiv.org/abs/2103.00020

17. Razavian, A.S., Azizpour, H., Sullivan, J., Carlsson, S.: CNN features off-the-shelf: an astounding baseline for recognition (2014). http://arxiv.org/abs/1403.6382

18. Settles, B.: Active learning literature survey (2009). https://burrsettles.com/pub/settles.activelearning.pdf

19. Yu, F., et al.: BDD100K: a diverse driving dataset for heterogeneous multitask learning (2018). http://arxiv.org/abs/1805.04687

A Survey of Data Challenges Across a Modernizing Bureaucracy: A New Perspective on Examining Old Government Problems

Andrew Bowne[1], Lindsey McEvoy[1], Dhruv Gupta[1], Cameron Brown[1], Vijay Gadepally[2], and El Kindi Rezig[2(✉)]

[1] United States Air Force, Washington, USA
{andrew.bowne.2,lindsey.mcevoy.1,dhruv.gupta,
cameron.brown.8}@us.af.mil
[2] Massachusetts Institute of Technology, Cambridge, USA
vijayg@ll.mit.edu, elkindi@mit.edu

Abstract. The introduction and increasing popularity of artificial intelligence (AI) and machine learning (ML) technologies allow organizations to gain valuable insights from their copious amounts of data. However, legacy organizations often struggle to overcome outdated data management practices and unleash the potential of AI and ML on their data. There is simply too much data to sift through manually. Therefore, a data science tool is required to locate relevant information effectively within an organizations' data lake. This paper presents a survey of challenges government organizations face related to this data discovery issue. The challenges are ubiquitous across mission sets, covering human resources and personnel management, logistics and supply chains, fraud and predatory business detection, government procurement, and civil litigation. This paper introduces the Data Discovery by Example (DICE) system to alleviate this problem. Unlike traditional data discovery techniques to find data of interest within a data lake, DICE alleviates the need to write queries and does not require users to manually inspect the lake to find their data of interest. Lastly, we walk through a DICE example, where we apply the tool on data from complaints of predatory business practices. This example highlights the challenges of acquiring, accessing, and interpreting data across multiple agencies and functions. There is an opportunity for innovative, ML-enabled data discovery solutions, such as DICE, to help unlock the value of data and augment development of a modern government organization.

Keywords: Data management · Procurement · Government · Human resources · Logistics · Fraud · Compliance

1 Introduction

Like most large legacy organizations, government organizations, possess mountains of data. With accelerating advancements of artificial intelligence (AI) and machine learning (ML), government organizations are increasingly looking to these emerging technologies

E. K. Rezig et al. (Eds.): DMAH 2022/Poly 2022, LNCS 13814, pp. 10–23, 2022.
https://doi.org/10.1007/978-3-031-23905-2_2

not only to boost economies and promote national security, but to simply manage and analyze copious data as well [1]. However, the application of AI to any new domain is a daunting task, and it is common for legacy organizations to struggle with overcoming data management practices that have existed long before AI and ML were seen as potential tools to gain insight and improve efficiency. While data is necessary for AI/ML systems to meet the intended outcome, the large volume of data possessed by government organizations are typically plagued by common problems [2]. Relevant data is often stored in disparate, "siloed" databases, requiring lengthy data wrangling, often with multiple custodians and lacking standardization or application programming interfaces (API) [1]. Thus, before government organizations can leverage AI and ML to extract insights into their data and increase efficiency, they must first overcome the barriers posed by legacy data management practices.

This paper presents a survey of real-world challenges that government organizations face in executing their duties. Although the challenges discussed herein originate in the United States, most of these challenges and lessons learned are ubiquitous for many large government agencies and organizations regardless of location, domain, or function. Several of these challenges were discussed in workshops with government officials from Australia and the United Kingdom, as well as private sector domain counterparts, confirming the transferability of these case studies outside the United States government and more generally to large, legacy bureaucracies in the throes of modernization.

The data challenges discussed in this paper involve a wide variety of government functions and are derived from multi-disciplinary perspectives. The government tasks highlighted include internal human resources and personnel management; logistics and supply chains; fraud detection within and outside the government; administrative and regulatory legal practice; government procurement; due diligence and regulatory compliance; and civil litigation. Each task is described in detail with a focus on the types of data managed, how the data is used, and any unique problems inherent in the government function that demand additional considerations about data management, such as privacy, proprietary, privilege, security, or legal requirement. Additionally, what data is required to perform the task and whether such data is readily available and usable for the intended purposes is also discussed. Finally, each case study summarizes the data challenge and constraints that must be overcome to accomplish the task.

2 Case Studies

The case studies presented below are real-world examples of data management challenges experienced in completing common government tasks. The five areas of discussion include vignettes from personnel management, logistics, fraud and predatory business practice detection, government procurement, and civil litigation.

2.1 Personnel Management Databases

Many large organizations maintain multiple databases to manage various personnel matters [3]. However, few organizations are as large or complex as the United States Air Force (USAF), with a total force of more than 689,000 personnel [4]. The USAF has multiple data systems to enter, update, retrieve, and maintain personnel information. Beyond the Department of Defense (DoD)-provided systems, the USAF, along with the other military services, has its own set of programs and applications as well as databases to recruit, assess, manage, train, develop, and track its personnel. Below are brief descriptions of several of the 140 programs databases of the USAF's personnel systems [5].

Defense Enrollment Eligibility Reporting System (DEERS). DEERS, the Defense Enrollment Eligibility Reporting System, is the DoD's method to verify and confirm the eligibility for the entirety of the Uniformed Service's benefits, including all active duty, retired, members of a Reserve component, United States-sponsored foreign military, other personnel as authorized by the DoD, and their eligible family members [6]. As a DoD-system, it is a top-down database that Air Force personnel are required to use and must update personal information changes, such as dependent family members through marriage, birth, adoption, or guardianship, throughout their careers. Registration in DEERS is required for healthcare benefits as well as command sponsorship for personnel permitted to reside in foreign countries under the applicable Status of Forces Agreement. The system is also used to forecast and allocate resources for buildings and staffing of installation hospitals, schools, and commissaries, as well as being the only system used for access granting on DoD premises via identification cards for authorized beneficiaries and common access cards (CAC) for military, civilian, and some contractor personnel.

milConnect. milConnect is also its own database maintained by the Defense Manpower Data Center (DMDC) [6]. It enables military members and their dependents to access their information, personnel records, health-care eligibility, and contacts. The data enabling this site resides on DEERS [6].

Assignment Management System (AMS). The Assignment Management System allows active-duty members to volunteer for future assignments, see vacancies and view at a copy of their personnel information [6]. AMS sources its personnel information from another database, the Military Personnel Data System [5], but it is its own database for managing and maintaining assignments.

myFSS. The "My Force Support Squadron" program has a suite of internal applications and databases such as myFITNESS, which manages and updates physical fitness and respective readiness statuses, and MyEval, the evaluation system that allows members and units to collaboratively build evaluations and rate them [6].

Task: Applying for or Identifying Candidates for a Special Duty. One common scenario is when a vacancy appears for a special duty. Special duties include a variety of positions, such as foreign exchange officer, general officer's aide, speechwriter, military attaché to a civilian agency, etc. Most special duties require specific knowledge, skills, or experience to be eligible. Sometimes, to determine whether a service member is eligible for a special duty, multiple programs and databases must be viewed. Depending on the database the relevant information is stored, either the member or the personnel making the assignment decision may have access; however sometimes only one side can access a relevant database. Because of this, many special duty assignment opportunities are not targeted to eligible candidates. This process ensures the widest dissemination of the opportunity, but because only a small percentage are eligible for any given opportunity, the many opportunities available become noise, and eligible members may not discover the opportunity before the deadline despite receiving a notice.

The Air Force recently begun efforts to modernize its personnel management programs. Improvements include auto-population of information residing on different databases and integration of various programs that had previously required manual data entry, saving both personnel and support staff time [7].

2.2 Supply Chain Logistics

Supply chains are critical to the success of any business. They encompass a network of everything involved in the production flow of goods and services. Inventory management is a key measure to ensuring the supply chain operates smoothly. Effective inventory management requires reliable technology to track, monitor and balance supply and demand. Ineffective inventory management can lead to increased costs, supply chain delays, excess, and spoilage. Furthermore, numerous disparate systems to manage inventory causes confusion, resource strain and reduced productivity due to retraining.

The Department of Defense (DoD) operates one of the largest and most complex logistics operations in the world. The DoD procures and manages inventories of spare and repair parts necessary to maintain mission readiness of all force structure elements. Within the DoD, the Department of the Air Force (DAF) spent over $1 billion in fiscal year 2022 to maintain an inventory of aircraft, missile, space, and other spare and repair parts [8]. The DAF operates a complex interconnected set of automated systems to determine inventory requirements, guide distribution of parts among bases and depots around the world, and track demand history and item characteristics of military assets.

ILS-S is the over-arching system built from several subsystems that support base-level supply chain management applications. It tracks over 35 million assets valued at $18 billion that are stored across 1.7 million warehouse locations [9]. ILS-S serves as a centralized way to access, order, track and disperse inventory. However, if, for example, an airman works in a supply shop that also services the F-35 Lightning II aircraft or issues personal protective equipment (PPE), they will need to learn and use ALIS/ODIN and/or DPAS respectively, to perform basic materiel management duties.

ALIS is the vast information-gathering system that was designed to support mission planning, supply chain management and maintenance. Currently, ODIN is replacing ALIS due to numerous system difficulties and shortfalls. ODIN includes a new logistics information system architecture to support international logistics and operational management of the global F-35 fleet [10]. With this ALIS to ODIN system replacement, logistics readiness airmen needed to relearn and access another data system.

DPAS is an additional asset management system designed to support all Federal and DoD property requirements [11]. It tracks and manages both accountable and non-accountable assets from acquisition and disposition [11]. With all these systems personnel need to connect and search different data sources one at a time to manage, track and order all parts.

ILS-S solved a lot of problems when it combined disparate systems. However, there are still several other logistics information systems that are utilized in tandem. Additionally, with the inevitable introduction of newer aircraft, parts, and technologies, there may come even more inventory management systems.

Task: Query Status of Parts Across Multiple Databases. The challenge to logisticians is the lack of an application to discover and retrieve inventory information through a simple query across all logistics systems without the nuances accompanied with each of them. Data discovery through join paths and organically through user provided examples could provide logistics readiness personnel a standardized service capable of identifying the nature, location, and retrieval path of the available inventory information across the DAF enterprise. This capability will enable logisticians, reduce operating costs, improve system flexibility and ensure full mission readiness across multiple installations.

2.3 Detecting and Preventing Fraud and Predatory Business Practices

Government organizations are subject to fraud and predatory business practices and the perpetrator can be outside or inside the government. Likewise, the victim can be the government itself, or vulnerable individuals working for the government, such as junior military members. Such crimes or civil complaints can be discovered and even prevented with sufficient data; however, obtaining such data in a timely, accessible, and useful manner has remained elusive.

Detecting and Preventing Fraud Against the Government. The United States federal government is expected to spend over $6 trillion in fiscal year 2022 [12]. While the defense department is the largest agency recipient of federal funding at over $750 billion, several trillion dollars have been paid to claimants for COVID-19 relief and economic stimulus [12]. The sheer size and the complexity of the agency programs creates a need for technology-based monitoring [12]. Effective controls of this massive budget include upfront preventive controls to reduce the possibility of fraud and detecting and monitoring claimants after payment of relief or stimulus fund [12]. Investigations and prosecutions of alleged fraud is costly and requires significant human resources [12]. However, at a time when the need for fraud detection increased, the various relief and stimulus packages were distributed through each state's IT systems, many of which were designed decades ago and lacked the capability to conduct data analysis or monitor abnormal transactions [12].

Detecting and Preventing Fraud and Predatory Business Practices Against Military Members. The operational readiness of military members is a national security priority. Readiness requires military members to avoid financial and legal problems that can distract from the mission. Accordingly, the United States has several laws that aim to provide additional protections against fraud and predatory business practices that can adversely impact mission readiness. These protections for military members and their families include the Service Members Civil Relief Act (SCRA) and the Military Lending Act (MLA), laws that prohibit fraud and other predatory business practices such as high interest rates on credit and loans, applying early termination charges on leases, or binding arbitration [13]. Additionally, military members and their dependents are entitled to legal assistance to aid in enforcing these protections [14].

However, as with fraud detection against the government, the best measure is to prevent the fraud or predatory practice before it requires legal intervention. The primary means available to an installation commander to prevent predatory business practices from degrading mission readiness is to establish "off-limits" restrictions, effectively ordering personnel within the command from entering or transacting with businesses that victimize military members and dependents [15]. Although commanders have substantial discretion to temporarily declare a business off-limits, there must be sufficient cause and due process procedures must be followed [15]. Thus, the command must have evidence of fraud or predatory business practices before establishing preventive measures. Without sufficient records of such practices, a business can assert that the decision to ban military personnel from transacting with it was arbitrary and capricious and sue the government for relief.

Task: Collect and Analyze Relevant Data to Prevent Military Members from Predatory Business Practices. Although it is common for commands to obtain anecdotal evidence of local violations of SCRA and MLA, often the evidence is insufficient to support the establishment of off-limits restrictions. While there is no database maintained by installations specific to complaints of fraud and predatory business practices, there are many such databases maintained by civilian jurisdictions at the municipal, country, state, and federal level. By obtaining these public records, and analyzing the complaints, business addresses, and proximity to military installations, commanders can derive sufficient insight to understand trends in predatory business tactics in the local area and prevent financial and legal issues amongst the personnel under their command. The challenge is each jurisdiction tracks such consumer complaints differently. Each database contains different columns of information, unique naming conventions, and use various data formats and table schema. Accordingly, even if a command obtained all relevant data from civilian jurisdictions, conducting data discovery and understanding the data would be prohibitively time consuming, especially as the civilian data does not indicate whether the complainant was a military member or dependent. For a commander to demonstrate sufficient cause to order off-limits restrictions, they would need to find multiple instances of fraud or other predatory business practices. They would then need to assess which of those practices are violations of the SCRA or the MLA if perpetrated against a military member or their family members in proximity to the installation and neighboring towns where many personnel reside.

The Department of the Air Force – Massachusetts Institute of Technology Artificial Intelligence Accelerator (AIA) researched this problem as a use case for a Data Discovery by Example (DICE) system [16]. Unlike traditional data discovery techniques to find data of interest within a data lake, DICE alleviates the need to write queries (which requires knowledge of the data lake structure) and it does not require users to manually inspect the lake to find their data of interest [16]. The research team (including several of the authors of this paper) collected many datasets from civilian consumer protection agencies and attorney general's offices that contain data on complaints of predatory business practices. It also collected various tables containing information about the location military installations. As the consumer protection tables typically represented the location of the business by town, street address, and/or postal code, and the military installation tables representing location by geographic coordinates, additional tables were required to convert geographic coordinates to postal codes. Once the relevant data was obtained, it was stored in a data lake to begin discovery through the DICE system.

The hypothesis was that if a commander obtained relevant information, i.e., data about potential SCRA and MLA violations, locations of businesses that received numerous complaints or substantiated allegations of fraud or predatory business practices, and the relative location of military installations, they could find businesses that operate in proximity of military personnel and their families that may have a proclivity for causing readiness issues. This information could then be used to find trends of problematic business practices in the area to issue general warnings to throughout the command or, if there is sufficient evidence to show cause, establish off-limits restrictions on specific businesses. However, this data lake is much too large to sift through manually. A data science tool is required to locate the relevant data effectively and efficiently within the data lake.

Like all data discovery, the DICE system is highly experimental and takes several iterations to produce a satisfactory data pipeline [16]. However, the command could start with providing example records of installation names (See Fig. 1).

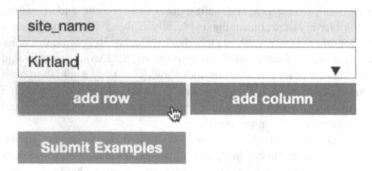

Fig. 1. DICE demonstration showing user-provided examples of military installation names.

A possible join path between tables related to installation names and the state the installation in located in could connect relevant data (See Fig. 2).

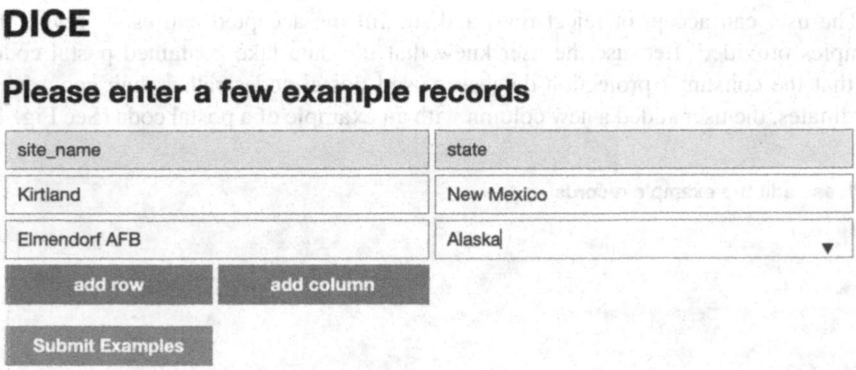

DICE

Please enter a few example records

site_name	state
Kirtland	New Mexico
Elmendorf AFB	Alaska

add row   **add column**

Submit Examples

Fig. 2. User-provided column with example records connecting installation name with state.

With those two columns created, the user can submit the user-provided examples to DICE. The DICE system provides additional data from the data lake that is semantically related to the examples. In the first iteration, DICE added more installation names with the states those installations are located in. Additionally, it provides a new column of geographic locations that were contained in the data lake (See Fig. 3).

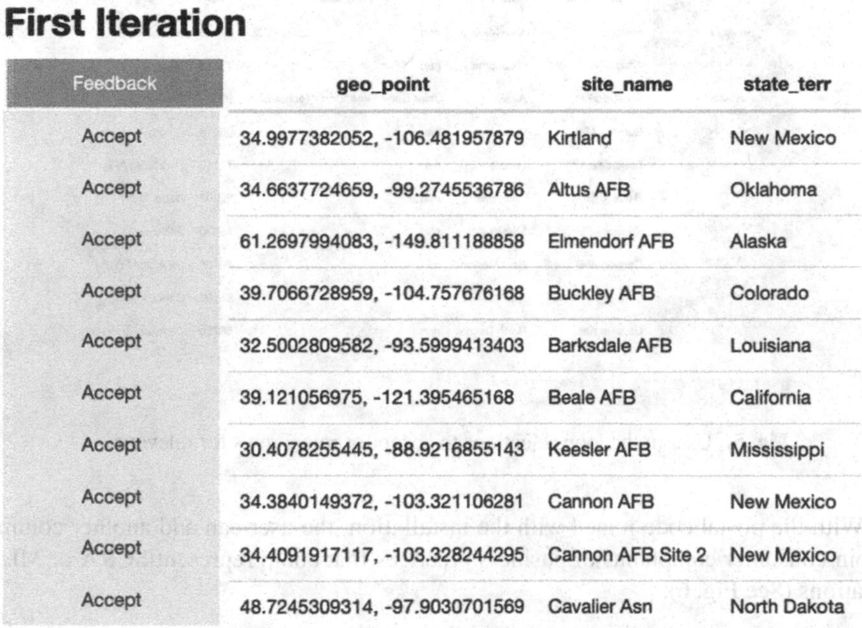

First Iteration

Feedback	geo_point	site_name	state_terr
Accept	34.9977382052, -106.481957879	Kirtland	New Mexico
Accept	34.6637724659, -99.2745536786	Altus AFB	Oklahoma
Accept	61.2697994083, -149.811188858	Elmendorf AFB	Alaska
Accept	39.7066728959, -104.757676168	Buckley AFB	Colorado
Accept	32.5002809582, -93.5999413403	Barksdale AFB	Louisiana
Accept	39.121056975, -121.395465168	Beale AFB	California
Accept	30.4078255445, -88.9216855143	Keesler AFB	Mississippi
Accept	34.3840149372, -103.321106281	Cannon AFB	New Mexico
Accept	34.4091917117, -103.328244295	Cannon AFB Site 2	New Mexico
Accept	48.7245309314, -97.9030701569	Cavalier Asn	North Dakota

Fig. 3. First iteration by DICE after user-submitted examples.

The user can accept or reject rows and submit the accepted entries, or revise the examples provided. Because the user knew that the data lake contained postal codes and that the consumer protection databases used postal codes rather than geographic coordinates, the user added a new column with an example of a postal code (See Fig. 4).

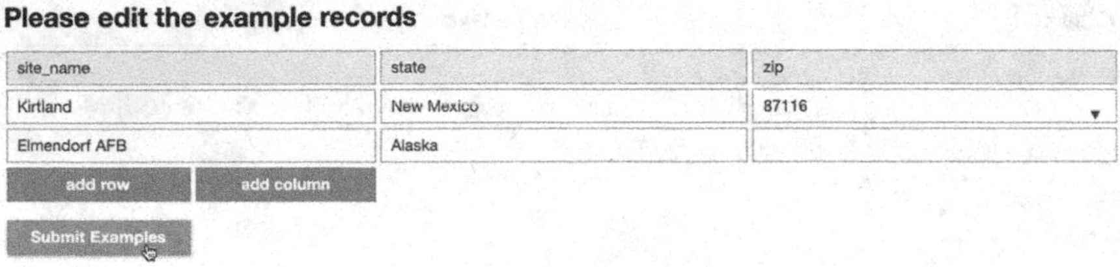

Please edit the example records

site_name	state	zip
Kirtland	New Mexico	87116
Elmendorf AFB	Alaska	

add row   add column

Submit Examples

Fig. 4. User-provided example of postal code of installation.

After submitting the postal code, DICE produces a second iteration that joined the postal codes and cities in addition to the installation name and state. The user can then accept the rows provided to refine the search (See Fig. 5) or continue revise examples.

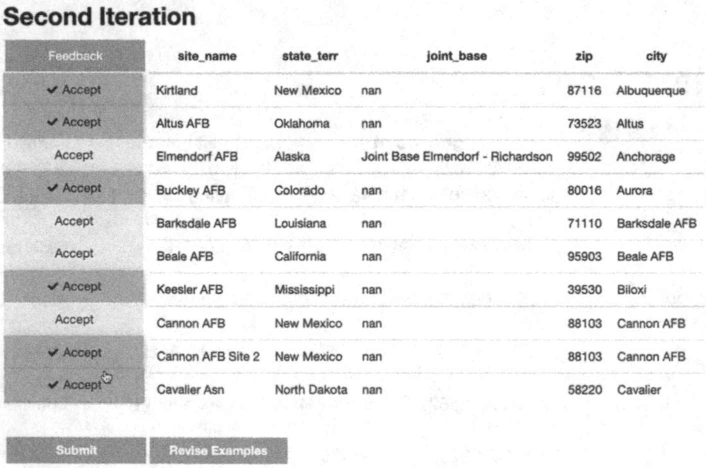

Second Iteration

Feedback	site_name	state_terr	joint_base	zip	city
✓ Accept	Kirtland	New Mexico	nan	87116	Albuquerque
✓ Accept	Altus AFB	Oklahoma	nan	73523	Altus
Accept	Elmendorf AFB	Alaska	Joint Base Elmendorf - Richardson	99502	Anchorage
✓ Accept	Buckley AFB	Colorado	nan	80016	Aurora
Accept	Barksdale AFB	Louisiana	nan	71110	Barksdale AFB
Accept	Beale AFB	California	nan	95903	Beale AFB
✓ Accept	Keesler AFB	Mississippi	nan	39530	Biloxi
Accept	Cannon AFB	New Mexico	nan	88103	Cannon AFB
✓ Accept	Cannon AFB Site 2	New Mexico	nan	88103	Cannon AFB
✓ Accept	Cavalier Asn	North Dakota	nan	58220	Cavalier

Submit   Revise Examples

Fig. 5. User in the loop selections to accept or reject rows for relevancy.

With the postal code joined with the installation, the user can add another column to join consumer complaints of business practices that could represent SCRA or MLA violations (See Fig. 6).

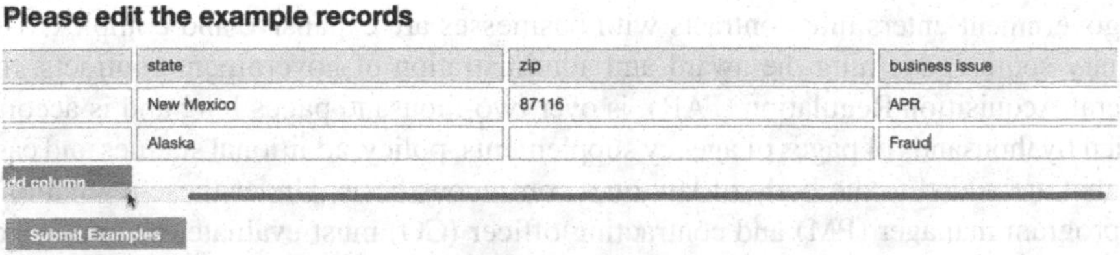

Please edit the example records

state	zip	business issue
New Mexico	87116	APR
Alaska		Fraud

add column

Submit Examples

Fig. 6. User-provided examples of business issues that could indicate violations of SCRA or MLA leading to military personnel readiness issues for the command.

The user can then submit examples and DICE joined additional tables from the data lake, provided the complaints of relevant predatory business practices and the company name the allegation was made against (See Fig. 7).

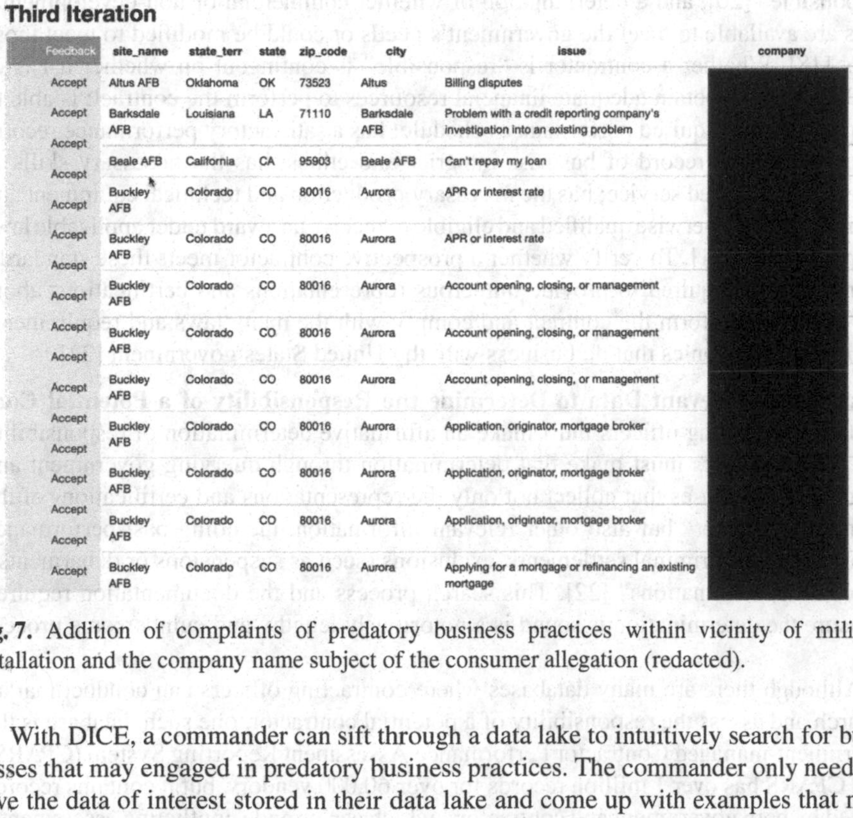

Third Iteration

Feedback	site_name	state_terr	state	zip_code	city	issue	company
Accept	Altus AFB	Oklahoma	OK	73523	Altus	Billing disputes	
Accept	Barksdale AFB	Louisiana	LA	71110	Barksdale AFB	Problem with a credit reporting company's investigation into an existing problem	
Accept							
Accept	Beale AFB	California	CA	95903	Beale AFB	Can't repay my loan	
Accept	Buckley AFB	Colorado	CO	80016	Aurora	APR or interest rate	
Accept	Buckley AFB	Colorado	CO	80016	Aurora	APR or interest rate	
Accept	Buckley AFB	Colorado	CO	80016	Aurora	Account opening, closing, or management	
Accept	Buckley AFB	Colorado	CO	80016	Aurora	Account opening, closing, or management	
Accept	Buckley AFB	Colorado	CO	80016	Aurora	Account opening, closing, or management	
Accept	Buckley AFB	Colorado	CO	80016	Aurora	Application, originator, mortgage broker	
Accept	Buckley AFB	Colorado	CO	80016	Aurora	Application, originator, mortgage broker	
Accept	Buckley AFB	Colorado	CO	80016	Aurora	Application, originator, mortgage broker	
Accept	Buckley AFB	Colorado	CO	80016	Aurora	Applying for a mortgage or refinancing an existing mortgage	

Fig. 7. Addition of complaints of predatory business practices within vicinity of military installation and the company name subject of the consumer allegation (redacted).

With DICE, a commander can sift through a data lake to intuitively search for businesses that may engaged in predatory business practices. The commander only needs to have the data of interest stored in their data lake and come up with examples that may lead to joining tables without the requirement to have knowledge of the structure of the data lake or ability to use special discovery tools [16].

2.4 Government Procurement

The United States government is the single largest customer in the world, spending over $500 billion on contracts in 2018 [17]. The laws, regulations, and policy that how the government enters into contracts with businesses are expansive and complex. The primary source governing the award and administration of government contracts, the Federal Acquisition Regulation (FAR), is over two-thousand pages long and is accompanied by thousands of pages of agency supplements, policy, additional statutes and case law that are added to the body of law on a continuous basis. Under these regulations, the program manager (PM) and contracting officer (CO) must evaluate the market for the service or good it anticipates buying in, and any of the potential competitors before awarding a contract [18].

Market Research and Due Diligence. There are several requirements that must be met to ensure the government meets its obligations to fairly and transparently compete an opportunity for a contract award [19] while ensuring that the government buyer obtains a good value for the goods or services it acquires. Several of those requirements include the obligation to conduct market research [18], that a prospective contractor is "responsible" [20], and a determination of whether commercial or non-developmental items are available to meet the government's needs or could be modified to meet those needs [18]. Whether a contractor is "responsible" is contingent on whether it has or has the ability to obtain adequate financial resources to perform the contract; is able to comply with the required performance schedule; has a satisfactory performance record; has a satisfactory record of business integrity and ethics; has the necessary skills to perform the required service; has the necessary production and technical equipment and facilities; and is otherwise qualified and eligible to receive an award under applicable laws and regulations [21]. To verify whether a prospective contractor meets these standards, contractors are required to provide numerous representations and certifications about their ability to perform the contract and comply with the many laws and requirements imposed on companies that do business with the United States government [22].

Task: Assess Relevant Data to Determine the Responsibility of a Potential Contractor Contracting officers must make an affirmative determination of responsibility [23]. These officers must make that determination through querying government and commercial databases that collect not only the representations and certifications of the potential contractor "but also other relevant information, including past performance history, civil and criminal settlements, exclusions (such as suspensions or debarments), and contract terminations" [22]. This search process and the documentation required to ensure the determination is sound is a notoriously lengthy and cumbersome process [22].

Although there are many databases where contracting officers can conduct market research and assess the responsibility of a potential contractor, one such database is the government-managed Contractor Performance Assessment Reporting System (CPARS) [24]. CPARS has over 1 million records for over 60,000 vendors, but it contains records created by both government and contractors, which can provide conflicting assessments. Additionally, CPARS data is so voluminous that it is challenging for contracting officers to find relevant data efficiently [22].

This important, yet challenging, task of reviewing voluminous data can be made easier with the assistance of machine learning tools. However, given the high cost of government contract and high stakes of the responsibility determination, it is critical that the data collection is robust, accurate, and complete [22].

2.5 Civil Litigation

Government agencies in the United States are required to preserve and ultimately produce information that may be relevant to a claim or defense raised in civil litigation. Pursuant to civil rules of procedure, the government has a duty to preserve and produce any non-privileged, potentially relevant information; present evidence – data that is relevant to the litigated matter, non-privileged, not overly prejudicial, and reliable (the data is authentic, and there is a chain of custody).

To satisfy this requirement, agencies often must rely heavily on self-collection, the process of individual custodians searching for and collecting their own information. Self-collection, however, is often disfavored by the courts and agencies routinely receive requests to conduct back-end, administrator searches. These requests often include search filters such as the identity of specific custodians, relevant date ranges, and search terms. Due to various factors, the administrators will only conduct an email search using custodian and date range as search filters. As a result, the requesting attorney often receives a large volume of information, most of which is not relevant.

Task: Review Large Volumes of Data for Potential Relevancy Using Both Linear Search Terms and More Dynamic Technology Assisted Review. Many federal agency litigation offices have the capability to process the data to apply search terms. However, this electronic discovery reference model (See Fig. 8), takes weeks, if not longer, to move from very large quantities of data to understanding what data is relevant to the litigation, responsive to the discovery request, and discoverable evidence under the rule of court [25].

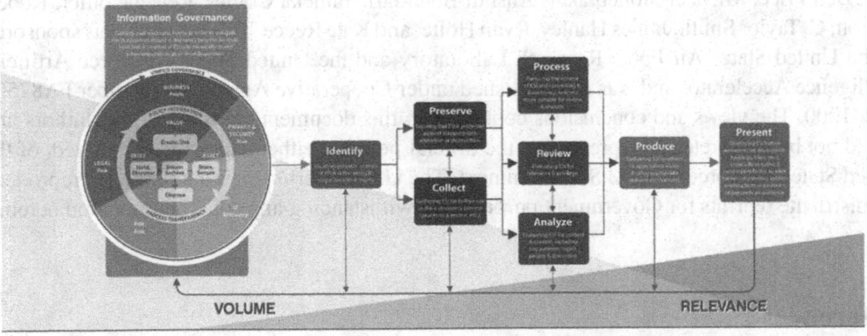

Fig. 8. The concept model used to sift through voluminous information to identify relevant evidence that can be produced and presented in court.

The stages of the model include information governance, identification of potential sources of electronically stored information, protecting such information from inappropriate alteration or destruction, and processing and reviewing raw data from dozens for different formats. Once the data is collected, the litigation team reduces the volume of data and, if necessary, converts the data to a format more suitable for review and analysis. The review of the data focused on identifying and classifying relevant evidence and information covered by privilege. While this process is a conceptual model, and not necessarily intended to be applied in as a linear process, it is helpful to organize and process the large volume of information that may be produced to the opposing party and presented in court as evidence [25]. However, following this process without technology assistance remains expensive and labor intensive.

This discovery model can be assisted through a variety of data management and machine learning-enhanced analytics tools. These tools can save time, expenses, and mitigate risk should discovery become an issues from initial creation of the electronically stored information through its final disposition [25].

3 Conclusion

These case studies illustrate the challenges of acquiring, accessing, and interpreting data across multiple government agencies and functions. While there are barriers to modernizing data management practices for more efficient and effective administration of government tasks, there is opportunity for innovative solutions. Developing data pipelines, standardization, and open systems can make data AI-ready, and thus, more useful. Advancements in ML-enabled data discovery tools, natural language processing, convolutional neural networks, and other algorithms can offer solutions to unlock the value of data and augment the development of a modern government administration.

Acknowledgements. The authors wish to acknowledge the following individuals for their contributions and support: Bob Bond, Jeremy Kepner, Tucker Hamilton, Garry Floyd, Mike Kanaan, Tim Kraska, Charles Leiserson, Christian Prothmann, John Radovan, Daniela Rus, Allan Vanterpool, Ben Price, Michael Stonebraker, Anshul Bhandari, Tameka Collier, Renee Collier, Robert Preston, C. Taylor Smith, James Hanley, Ryan Holte, and Kate Reece. This research was sponsored by the United States Air Force Research Laboratory and the United States Air Force Artificial Intelligence Accelerator and was accomplished under Cooperative Agreement Number FA8750–19-2–1000. The views and conclusions contained in this document are those of the authors and should not be interpreted as representing the official policies, either expressed or implied, of the United States Air Force or the U.S. Government. The U.S. Government is authorized to reproduce and distribute reprints for Government purposes notwithstanding any copyright notation herein.

References

1. Newman, J.: Toward AI security: global aspirations for a more resilient future. University of California, Berkeley, Center for Long-Term Cybersecurity, 21, 24, 30, 34 (2019)
2. Koumpan, E.: 13 Tips & techniques to use when visualizing data. benelux intelligence community. https://www.bi-kring.nl/component/easytagcloud/293-module/120-data-analytics. Accessed 25 Sept 2022
3. Vrontis, D., et al.: Artificial intelligence, robotics, advanced technologies and human resource management: a systematic review. Int. J. Hum. Resour. Manag. 33(6), 1237–1266 (2021)

4. United States air force. https://www.af.mil/About-Us/. Accessed 25 Sept 2022
5. Gross, C.: MilPDS upgrade successful. https://www.buckley.spaceforce.mil/News/Article-Display/Article/322518/milpds-upgrade-successful/. Accessed 28 Sept 2022
6. Air force personnel center. https://www.afpc.af.mil/Career-Management/. Accessed 25 Sept 2022
7. Secretary of the air force public affairs: DAF to launch myEval in 2022. https://www.af.mil/News/Article-Display/Article/2892242/daf-to-launch-myeval-in-2022/. Accessed 28 Sept 2022
8. Department of defense budget fiscal year 2023. https://comptroller.defense.gov/Portals/45/Documents/defbudget/FY2023/FY2023_p1.pdf. Accessed 25 Sept 2022
9. Business and enterprise systems directorate: modern logistics system aids, tracks air force inventory. Air force. https://www.af.mil/News/Article-Display/Article/2891103/modern-logistics-system-aids-tracks-air-force-inventory/. Accessed Accessed 25 Sept 2022
10. F-35 Joint Program Office: F-35 Joint Program Office completes initial deployment of new, improved logistics hardware. Edwards Air Force Base. https://www.edwards.af.mil/News/Article/2919347/f-35-joint-program-office-completes-initial-deployment-of-new-improved-logistic/ Accessed 25 Sept 2022
11. Defense Property Accountability System https://dpassupport.golearnportal.org/index.php/system-solutions-dpas/by-business-need/140-dpas-overview Accessed 25 Sept 2022
12. West, D.M.: Using AI and machine learning to reduce government fraud. Brookings, https://www.brookings.edu/research/using-ai-and-machine-learning-to-reduce-government-fraud/. Accessed 29 Sept 2022
13. Meister, L., et al.: Servicemember financial protection: a overview of key federal laws and regulations. Consum. Compliance Outlook **2**, 10–19 (2017)
14. Air Force Instruction 51–304, Legal Assistance, Notary, Preventive Law, and Tax Programs (2018)
15. CFR § 631.11, Off-limits establishments and areas
16. Rezig, E., et al.: Examples are all you need: iterative data discovery by example in data lakes. In: 12th Annual Conference on Innovative Data Systems Research, Chaminade, USA (2022)
17. Girth, A. M., Snider, K. F.: Acquisition in U.S. federal agencies: evidence from the world's largest buyer. J. Strateg. Contracting Negot. **4**(1–2), 3–5 (2020)
18. U.S.C. § 3306(a)(1)(B) (2018)
19. U.S.C. § 3101 et seq. (2018)
20. U.S.C. §§ 3702(b), 3703(c) (2018)
21. Federal Acquisition Regulation 9.104–1
22. Tillipman, J.: Using AI to Reduce Performance Risk in U.S. Procurement. The Regulatory Review (2022). https://www.theregreview.org/2022/06/29/tillipman-using-ai-to-reduce-performance-risk-in-u-s-procurement/
23. Federal Acquisition Regulation 9.103(b)
24. Contractor Performance Assessment Reporting System. https://cpars.gov/. Accessed 30 Sept 2022
25. Electronic Discovery Reference Model. https://edrm.net/edrm-model/. Accessed 30 Sept 2022

Purpose Scan: A Purpose-Aware Access Method

Francisco D. B. S. Praciano, Paulo R. P. Amora[✉], Ítalo C. Abreu,
and Javam C. Machado

Universidade Federal do Ceará, Fortaleza, CE, Brazil
{daniel.praciano,paulo.amora,italo.abreu,javam.machado}@lsbd.ufc.br

Abstract. In this paper, we attack the problem of querying personal data according to related purposes. Our approach allows for specifying, in a SQL manner, the purpose of use to personal data. We define a new access method operator introduced in query plans to automatically enforce the purposes of data involved in a SQL query. Experimental results show that our method outperforms a view-based approach competitor.

1 Introduction

Personal data have become a first-class citizen in the domain of user applications. As a result, government bodies have acted to tilt this power dynamic to a balance, empowering users by providing rights over any ceded data. Legislations such as Europe's General Data Protection Regulation (GDPR) [10], California's Consumer Privacy Act (CCPA) [4], and Brazil's Lei Geral de Proteção de Dados (LGPD) [14] are all examples of that government action. A common ground on all these regulations is that the user who provides the data must accept, in a well-informed manner, for what purpose applications may process their data. From the data perspective, this consent can be understood as: only specific applications can use this personal data. Namely, we call this type of data access *purpose-aware access*, because applications that wish to consume this data must state their purpose to access, and the user must have accepted this type of usage.

Database Management Systems (DBMS) usually store data collected by online applications. Thus, a set of rule-based access and views, mechanisms already existent in current DBMS can solve the problem of purpose-aware access. Nevertheless, these types of solutions underperform because they introduce a processing overhead to each query since the DBMS must check the returned data for each query and client.

This problem is well discussed in academia, with works like [1,2,17] that discuss solutions for purpose-based access control. More recently, with the legal support provided by new regulations, new works such as [7,15,20] model purpose-based access control to abide by regulations. The works mentioned above provide purpose-based access control through query rewriting, either inside the DBMS, by the usage of stored procedures, or through middlewares, which fit between

E. K. Rezig et al. (Eds.): DMAH 2022/Poly 2022, LNCS 13814, pp. 24–36, 2022.
https://doi.org/10.1007/978-3-031-23905-2_3

the DBMS and other applications. However, it is possible to access data through usual operators, and access paths, i.e., a scan operator applied directly to the relation retrieves all data, then further operations are applied to ensure compliance with the purpose-based access rules. This either allows for an attacker to query directly the database bypassing the interface or obtain this data by inspecting unnecessary data loaded in memory.

We identify that this unprotected gap can be filled if only a special operator can access relations containing personal data. Furthermore, many of these solutions require that the DBMS user explicitly claim their access purpose within the query for the solution to rewrite it in a valid SQL query, adding constraints to it. This brings another issue, which is leaving identification to the data analyst. Ideally, a DBMS must be transparent in this regard, first, to guarantee that whoever queries the system remain ignorant of this additional layer within it. Second, to allow previous queries and procedures unaltered, avoiding rework to use the new system.

We added Purpose Scan as a leaf operator in the execution tree to ensure that only allowed data is returned. Other approaches bring this processing upwards in the tree, by using query rewriting or validating tuples after the scans are done (e.g. joining with other tables). Although both approaches are successful from the perspective of a user that only receives the final result, we believe that purpose enforcement should be at the lowest level to avoid any type of interference that may provide an user with inappropriate data outside of the DBMS.

In this work, we introduce a purpose-aware query processing module for relational DBMS compliant with data protection legislation, acting within query processing without exposing itself to users. In summary, the main contributions of this work are: In Sect. 2, we formalize a purpose modeling to ground our approach. In Sect. 3, we define Purpose Scan, a data access operator that performs purpose-aware scans and the corresponding approach to introduce it to query execution plans automatically, followed by an experimental analysis in Sect. 4 and related work discussion in Sect. 5.

2   Purpose Concept and Modeling

From a data access perspective, purpose can be understood as to how someone intends to process data. Given the new regulations and privacy concerns, anyone should not access all data equally since users have rights regarding whether their data should be used to a specific end. Through this perspective, we can characterize data in two ways: non-personal data, which can be accessed without any restriction or rule set, and personal data, which have access purposes assigned to it and may only be accessed by complying with purpose-aware access. In this work, we focus on personal data management and access. In this viewpoint, we can define three entities, inspired by GDPR [10]:

Data Owner: The party who provides the data. This data can reveal sensitive information about them. Consequently, the DBMS and whoever controls the data must handle it more carefully than other information. They have all rights pertaining to data processing and usage and may object to this use.

Data Processor: The party who intends to process data from the Data Owners. They must clearly state what ends they will use the retrieved data and how they will consume it.

Data Controller: The party who stores the data collected from Data Owners and provide them to Data Processors. Laws and regulations require that they comply with the Owners' wishes regarding data processing and usage. According to the Owners' requests, they manage the access permissions of personal data, actively allowing or denying access to data.

These entities are usually distinct, i.e., there is no organizational connection between the Data Owner, Controller, and Processor. There may be instances where the Controller and Processor may be within the same organization, but the more general case is that they are distinct. Data Controller configures the existing purposes whenever the Data Owner provides data to the Data Controller (e.g., sign up for a service, allow the Data Controller to read stored cookies). Once these consents are submitted, the Data Controller assigns the accepted purposes to the data. The purpose creation process requires active intervention by a Database Administrator (DBA). However, the Data Controller can perform the assignment automatically, be it through the DBA or a configured DBMS.

When the Data Processor queries Data Controller's DBMS, the DBMS links a preconfigured purpose to the Data Processor. The Data Controller configures this process before the Data Processor connection, so, whenever a given Data Processor connects, the DBMS grants their processing purposes and states them in the connection context. From this connection, be it a query tool or an API, the Data Processor can pose queries against the DBMS. The DBMS processes the query and uses the purpose metadata to enforce purpose-based access control over any personal data queried by the Data Processor. Therefore, only data from Data Owners that consented to the processing purpose will be returned to the Data Processor. We propose that the DBMS manages this purpose enforcement process, avoiding any human intervention and interaction. To the data analyst querying the database, this enforcement happens transparently. There are no changes in connecting to the database or querying data.

In this way, there is a design decision to how this model and approach change query results. When a query would violate consent, the DBMS may either abort the query or return a subset of request data that contains only data allowed for the provided purpose. Our approach strives for returning as much data as possible because aborting queries is too detrimental to the DBMS overall usage, especially when considering multiple purposes and entities. From these relationships, we can establish some definitions used throughout this work.

Definition 1. *A purpose is a finality in which data will be processed, e.g., Sales, Advertisement, Business Intelligence.*

Definition 2. *Assigned Purpose (AP) is the stated purpose that the Data Owner allows their data usage. APs are managed by the Data Controller. APs are assigned to a data instance (relation, tuple), and a data instance may have more than one AP.*

Definition 3. *Processing Purposes (PP) are the declared ends for which the Data Processor intends to use personal data. The Data Processor declares these upon requesting data from the Data Controller.*

Therefore, to consider a DBMS implementation of that purpose verification function, it must comply with the following claims:

Claim 1. *Personal data, which is data provided by a Data Owner, is stored as tuples in one or more relations and has one or more associated AP. Each AP must be consented individually.*

Claim 2. *A Data Processor must state their PP to access personal data.*

Claim 3. *If a relation contains any personal data, only purpose-aware access is allowed. An access path must ensure that only data where the PP set matches the AP set is returned.*

Claim 4. *If access is attempted to Personal Data and the PP does not match the data's AP, access is denied.*

Whenever a tuple has an AP, it means that only applications with the matching PP can access this tuple. In a relation, we may have several tuples, each with its own APs. Therefore, the relation's AP must be at least a union of all the tuple APs. A relation can also have APs unrelated to their tuples, meaning that every tuple in the relation that does not have an AP is accessible through the relation AP.

3 Purpose Enforcement

To restrict the data used to generate the query response to only those that $PP \subseteq AP$, we have added Purpose Scan in the list of available access methods. In this new access method, the APs associated with the data are checked against PPs before retrieving the data. This prevents data that is not allowed for a specific Data Processor to be used during processing and avoids the unnecessary cost of bringing it from disk to main memory.

Purpose Guarantee: To achieve purpose guarantee, Purpose Scan contains an empty list of which heap pages should the operator read from disk. Assuming a structure that gives us information about which relations or tuples have APs, the Purpose Scan starts filling this list with the data returned by that structure. This information must be a unique identifier in the relational context, at least in a relation scope. This identifier, called tuple id, can be formed by both the page id and the offset of the tuple within the respective page. In this way, Purpose Scan is able to identify the pages of the heap that should be read from disk and which tuples should be transferred to the rest of the plan. This work uses a filter structure, similar to Stacked Filters [6], that receives as input a single element. Therefore, we transform the tuple id composed of two numbers (page id and offset) into a single number by merging the bits of each of those numbers. Furthermore, it is essential to note that this transformation is bijective. That is, for each number generated, there is one and only one corresponding tuple id and vice versa. Thus, it is possible to find out which tuple id a given filter element represents and it also ensures that only those tuple ids inserted into the filter are actually returned. Once that list is created and filled, Purpose Scan is ready to start running. This same initial procedure is also performed in the Purpose Index Scan.

During the evaluation of the query plan, Purpose Scan executes similarly to the full table scan, except that only the tuples previously identified through that filter structure mentioned above are retrieved from the disk and passed on to the next operator. In other words, the tuples passed along have the respective PPs present in the query. The Purpose Index Scan, on the other hand, performs similarly to the index scan, with the difference that, among the tuples selected by the index, only those that are identified in the filter structure will be retrieved and forwarded to the next operator. To exemplify this, assume that there are three relations $R(a, b)$, $S(b, c)$, $T(c, d)$ with only relations R and T having sensitive data and consider the two execution plans shown in Fig. 1 for the following query:

```
SELECT R.a FROM R, S, T WHERE R.a = T.c AND S.b = T.c
AND S.b > 10 AND S.b < 19 AND T.c > 1
```

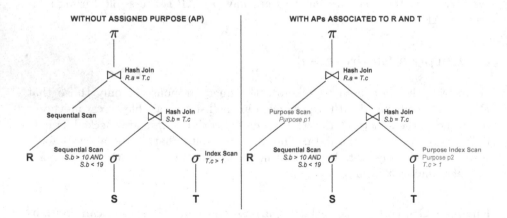

Fig. 1. Two execution plans for the same query, with and without purposes.

On the left side of the Fig. 1, we have a default execution plan considering that the relations have no associated APs. Hence, the access methods are those already known, for example, sequential scan on R and S, while index scan for T. On the right side, we show the execution plan for the query assuming that relation R is authorized for purpose $p1$ and, likewise, T is authorized for $p2$. Consequently, for these two relations, the Purpose Scan and the Purpose Index Scan, respectively, are the chosen access methods to guarantee that only data that have purposes $p1$ and $p2$ in relations R and T, respectively, are retrieved and forwarded to other operators. Finally, it is relevant to note that the method of accessing relation S remains the same as the previous one since this relation has no associated APs, probably because its data is not sensitive.

Integration with Query Processing Stack: The query processing stack is traditionally separated into four modules in a standard DBMS: Parser, Planner, Optimizer, and Executor [9]. These four modules together perform all the necessary operations to form the result of the queries. To illustrate how to integrate Purpose Scan into an existing commercial DBMS, we present in Fig. 2 the traditional query processing stack along with the changes required for its integration. On the one hand, Purpose Scan does not impact two modules during the entire query lifetime, Parser and Optimizer, which the blue boxes in the figure represent, so their logic remains completely unchanged. On the other hand, the Planner and Executor modules, the green ones in the figure, are the most affected by the changes brought by Purpose Scan. As can be seen in Fig. 2, Purpose Scan is only used when the data that is involved in the query has associated APs.

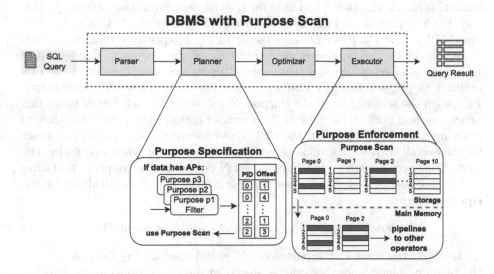

Fig. 2. Integration of purpose scan in DBMS.

To check if there are any purposes associated to tables or tuples, the operator has a hash-based data structure that verifies if some tuples of a given relation have at least one associated AP and if the PPs associated with the context of the user who submitted the query match these APs. Furthermore, this same data structure also makes it possible to find the correct structure storing purpose data. It is important to say that each structure is related to only one purpose. Purpose p1 Filter in Fig. 2 is used to identify which tuples in the relation are authorized to be processed for the corresponding filter purpose. The operator performs the necessary settings, such as retrieving a list of all tuple ids, page id - PID and offset, to make the Purpose Scan ready to be used in the next query processing steps.

Lastly, in the Executor module, we mainly changed to the Purpose Scan execution logic. This logic was incorporated as an Executor's sub-module named Purpose Enforcement. During run-time, Purpose Scan uses the data that has been configured in Planner to identify the heap pages that are read from Storage (usually from disk) and bring them into main memory. Then the Purpose Scan pipelines the tuples that satisfy the processing purposes for the other operators in the execution plan. For example, in Fig. 2 we have that only pages 0 and 2 are read from disk and brought to main memory and, afterward, tuples 1 and 4 of page 0 and 1, 3 of page 2 are forwarded to the other operators to generate the final result of the query. In short, this new sub-module encapsulate all these operations, and its integration takes place through the Volcano interface [11].

Cost of Purpose Scan. For the Purpose Scan to be used by the optimizer, the cost of this access method must be estimated so that the overall cost of the execution plan is calculated and used for the query optimization process. In this way, the first part of the Purpose Scan cost is to identify which data whose APs match PPs. The $PurposeCheck_{cost}$ factor in Eq. 1 represents that part which is dependent on the type of storage structure of the purposes. Besides, since Purpose Scan fetches all pages that contain tuples that have consent to the PPs and not all pages necessarily have qualifying tuples, i.e., have APs that match PPs, then the second part of the Purpose Scan cost is the number of times this access method performs a random IO access to transfer the pages from disk to main memory. In this context, the CPU cost of Purpose Scan has little impact on the overall cost, so this value is not taken into account when calculating the cost of this access method. In summary, let N be the number of pages that have tuples qualified for a given PP, then the Purpose Scan cost is calculated by the equation below:

$$PurposeScan_{cost} = PurposeCheck_{cost} + N \times RandIO_{cost} \qquad (1)$$

In Eq. 1, the value of the parameter N is obtained during the execution of the planning phase since this value is stored in the purpose metadata. In other words, N is the difference between the total number of pages in the relation being accessed and the number of pages with at least one qualified tuple whose APs match PPs. Calculating this value is possible because both are available at planning time in the database metadata. Furthermore, $PurposeCheck_{cost}$ is a known value based on how the purposes are stored and $RandIO_{cost}$ is a configurable DBMS parameter representing the cost of performing a random IO operation, and there is usually a default value for this knob.

Finally, it is worth highlighting the best and worst-case scenarios for the Purpose Scan cost. The best case is when all the qualifying tuples are concentrated on contiguous pages. Thus, a sequential IO access only reads that sub-part of the pages containing those tuples. In contrast, the worst case occurs when the qualifying tuples are spread across all pages, making it necessary to read all relation pages. In this case, the Purpose Scan costs are similar to doing a sequential scan or, respectively, index scan.

Cost of Purpose Index Scan. Similarly, the cost of the Purpose Index Scan is estimated using Eq. 2:

$$PurposeIndexScan_{cost} = Index_{cost} + PurposeCheck_{cost} + M \times RandIO_{cost} \quad (2)$$

Since Purpose Index Scan uses an underlying index to find pages that have tuples that satisfy a given predicate, then the cost for doing so is represented by the $Index_{cost}$ factor that appears at the beginning of the Eq. 2. The value of this factor will depend on the type of index. For example, for B+ tree, we will have that this factor is the cost of traversing the tree until finding the leaves that have tuples that satisfy the predicate, including the cost of accessing those leaves.

After selecting the leaves in the usual way, Purpose Index Scan will start accessing the pages selected by the index. However, as in Purpose Scan, only those pages that have at least one tuple whose APs match PPs will be accessed. Thus, $PurposeCheck_{cost}$ represents the cost of performing this check and let M be the number of pages selected by the index on which at least one tuple has consent for the purpose of the query. Therefore, $PurposeCheck_{cost}$ plus M multiplied by $RandIO_{cost}$ will be the complementary factor of the $Index_{cost}$ that appears in Eq. 2. Finally, we have that the value of M is available at the time of generating the plan and, in addition, the best and worst case remains the same as in the Purpose Scan mentioned above.

4   Experimental Evaluation

Setup. To build Purpose Scan, we used PostgreSQL version 9.6, adding it as an extension. Experiments were run in a Dell Power Edge machine with an Intel Xeon E5-2609 v3 1.9 GHz, 6 cores, running Ubuntu 18.04 and using a 7.2K RPM hard disk as storage technology. We used YCSB with factor 1, 000 as a benchmark through the OLTPBench [8]. The benchmark was set up to run for 10 min on each run.

Effectiveness. In the first experiment, we observed how effective Purpose Scan is regarding the number of tuples retrieved to generate the final query result considering purpose based access. In this scenario, the best outcome is that only allowed tuples are retrieved. Figure 3 shows the result obtained by the standard PostgreSQL to retrieve the tuples when varying the opt-in percentage between 10% to 100%. For 10% opt-in, we have that 10% of the retrieved tuples are allowed, while the other 90% are tuples that were retrieved unnecessarily. This situation occurs for both sequential scan and index scan. Note that up to 50% of opt-in, the amount of tuples retrieved and discarded is greater than that of retrieved and processed, which generates an unnecessary waste of resources. Obviously, for 100% opt-in, we have that PostgreSQL is total effective since all tuples are allowed.

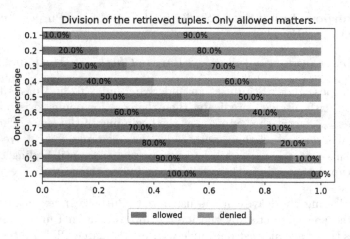

Fig. 3. Retrieved tuples separated into allowed and denied tuples when using Stock PostgreSQL.

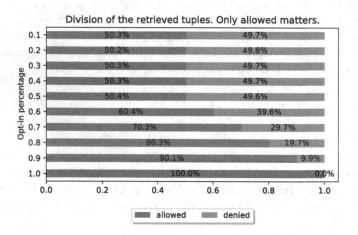

Fig. 4. Retrieved tuples separated into allowed and denied tuples when using PostgreSQL with Purpose Scan.

Likewise, Fig. 4 shows the result obtained by the Purpose Scan. To generate the result, we made the opt-in tuples spread across the pages with a probability of 50%, because when the opt-in tuples are clustered, Purpose Scan has full effectiveness, that is, only opt-in tuples are retrieved. With that, note that the Purpose Scan is more effective in retrieving tuples when opt-in percentage varies between 0.1 and 0.5. In these cases, Purpose Scan manages to balance the amount of tuples retrieved and discarded with those processed. Therefore, we can conclude that the more clustered the opt-in tuples are, the more effective the Purpose Scan will be. This same conclusion is also valid for the Purpose Index Scan.

Finally, to demonstrate the impact that Purpose Scan's effectiveness has, look at Fig. 5 which shows the number of IOs performed by PostgreSQL and Purpose Scan to retrieve the tuples. See that Purpose Scan can reduce the number of IOs, especially when the amount of opt-in is between 10% and 50%.

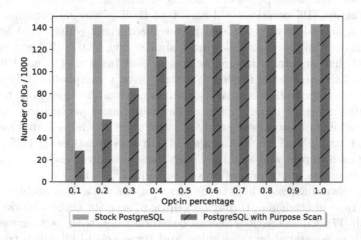

Fig. 5. Number of IOs when varying the percentage of opt-ins in both approaches.

Performance. In this experiment, we compare how Purpose Scan fares against an alternative method of ensuring purpose-based access. For this test, we intended to use both a view-based approach and row security policies, however, row security only works with tuples of 8 kB maximum size. As the tuples on YCSB surpass that limit, we are unable to perform the comparison. To perform the experiment, we remove access to the relation in the baseline and create a view containing the same subset of tuples that the purpose-aware system returns, i.e. the result set is the same in Purpose Scan and the view. The terminals query the relation and filters in Purpose Scan and query only the view in the baseline. Table 1 presents the completed requests between Purpose Scan and the view-based approach. The results show that our strategy outperforms a more traditional view-based approach by more than 48%, showing that there is not a trade-off between security and performance.

Table 1. Completed requests per terminal for each strategy.

Technique	Run 1	Run 2	Run 3	Average
View-based	1202	1209	1196	1202.3
Purpose Scan	1783	1785	1790	1786.0

5 Related Work

The need for trustworthy database systems technologies is urgent, as stated by Rogers et al. [18], and regulatory compliance recently became a high-interest theme in data management [5,13,22] and DBMSs, with works such as SchengenDB [12], which brings concepts on how a system may implement a regulation compliant end-to-end system, providing an overview on how to ensure adherence to principles such as purpose-aware access and delete guarantees. Compliance by Construction [19] describes a different method of storing personal data in user shards, accessible only through materialized views constructed according to the consumer application. Following a similar line, PODS [21] is a new data flow model that maintains internal states of pod tasks that control both the requests and the processing needed to ensure privacy-compliance. GDPRBench [20] provides a view on how regulatory compliance modifications done to a stock system without regard to any optimization cause many performance decreases and space allocation increases, justifying why more specialized approaches are necessary. Finally, Machado and Amora [3] survey impacts on DBMS systems, discussing each impact and existing approaches to address each one, providing general pointers on important aspects of possible solutions.

Purpose-aware access, which is the scope of our work, is a problem present for a long time in academia, through an optic of security access. Works such as Rizvi et al. [17], which rewrites queries based on rules, with data accesses done through views generated by these rules, and Byun and Li [2] which treats purposes as hierarchical entities, establishing operators to transition between these. Data Capsule [23], which describes an access method to personal data, with privacy guarantees to the retrieved data, and Sieve [15] defines a middleware which receives queries as input and, through a set of user defined functions and additional data stored in the database, rewriting queries to respect established access policies. On the topic of query rewriting, PriSQL [16] alters standard SQL language to add statements that allow the querier to establish query purpose within the query, Agrawal et al. [1] develops a permission-based access model similar to row security. Sypse [7] proposes the separation of personal data through pseudonymization and partitioning.

Our work mainly differs from existing approaches on the basis of data access. By bringing purpose verification to data retrieval from storage media, we avoid any possible data breach from outside the DBMS. Another upside is the transparent usage of this solution, in two ways: first, since no modifications are done to query parsing, DBMS usage remains the same for SQL queries; second, given that it is a modular approach in the sense that query processing essentially remains the same, only modifying the operator in a leaf node of the query plan, substituting a scan, therefore, it becomes compatible with other operators that use scans as underlying operations, such as joins, projections, among others. This transparent usage allows for composing this solution with others, to achieve a system that complies with more regulations, not only purpose-aware access.

6 Conclusion and Future Work

This work presents Purpose Scan, a new purpose-aware scan operator for query processing. This new operator works in conjunction with the others to have only opted personal data to be retrieved by the DBMS, complying with the current legislation. In this context, Purpose Scan outperforms a view-based access approach by almost 50% throughput, and has greater effectiveness in retrieving authorized tuples. A secondary effect is the possibility of making data completely unavailable, through a special assignment of purpose, achieving the right to be forgotten. Future works may address more requirements brought by these regulations, such as efficient auditing, delete guarantees and effective personal data representation.

Acknowledgements. This research was partially supported by CAPES (grant 88887.609129/2021) and LSBD/UFC.

References

1. Agrawal, R., Bird, P., Grandison, T., Kiernan, J., Logan, S., Rjaibi, W.: Extending relational database systems to automatically enforce privacy policies. In: ICDE, pp. 1013–1022. IEEE Computer Society, Tokyo (2005)
2. Byun, J., Li, N.: Purpose based access control for privacy protection in relational database systems. VLDB J. **17**(4), 603–619 (2008)
3. de Castro Machado, J., Amora, P.R.P.: How can DB systems be ready for privacy regulations. In: SBBD, pp. 235–240. SBC (2020)
4. CCPA: California Consumer Privacy Act. https://oag.ca.gov/privacy/ccpa (2018). Accessed 07 Oct 2021
5. Cohn-Gordon, K., et al.: DELF: safeguarding deletion correctness in online social networks. In: Capkun, S., Roesner, F. (eds.) 29th USENIX Security Symposium, USENIX Security 2020, 12–14 August 2020, pp. 1057–1074. USENIX Association (2020)
6. Deeds, K., Hentschel, B., Idreos, S.: Stacked filters: learning to filter by structure. Proc. VLDB Endow. **14**(4), 600–612 (2021)
7. Deshpande, A.: Sypse: privacy-first data management through pseudonymization and partitioning. In: CIDR, pp. 1–8 (2021). https://www.cidrdb.org/
8. Difallah, D.E., Pavlo, A., Curino, C., Cudré-Mauroux, P.: Oltp-bench: an extensible testbed for benchmarking relational databases. PVLDB **7**(4), 277–288 (2013). http://www.vldb.org/pvldb/vol7/p277-difallah.pdf
9. Elmasri, R., Navathe, S.B.: Fundamentals of Database Systems, 3rd edn. Addison-Wooley Longman, Cambridge (2000)

10. Regulation, G.D.P.: Regulation (EU) 2016/679 of the European Parliament and of the Council of 27 April 2016 on the protection of natural persons with regard to the processing of personal data and on the free movement of such data, and repealing Directive 95/46. Off. J. Eur. Union **59**, 1–88 (2016)
11. Graefe, G.: Volcano - an extensible and parallel query evaluation system. IEEE Trans. Knowl. Data Eng. **6**(1), 120–135 (1994)
12. Kraska, T., Stonebraker, M., Brodie, M., Servan-Schreiber, S., Weitzner, D.: SchengenDB: a data protection database proposal. In: Gadepally, V., et al. (eds.) DMAH/Poly -2019. LNCS, vol. 11721, pp. 24–38. Springer, Cham (2019). https://doi.org/10.1007/978-3-030-33752-0_2
13. Lehmann, A.: Scrambledb: oblivious (chameleon) pseudonymization-as-a-service. Proc. Priv. Enhancing Technol. **2019**(3), 289–309 (2019)
14. LGPD: Lei Geral de Proteção de Dados (2018). http://www.planalto.gov.br/ccivil_03/_ato2015-2018/2018/lei/L13709compilado.htm. Accessed 07 Oct 2021
15. Pappachan, P., Yus, R., Mehrotra, S., Freytag, J.: Sieve: a middleware approach to scalable access control for database management systems. Proc. VLDB Endow. **13**(11), 2424–2437 (2020)
16. Pun, S.: Prisql: a privacy preserving sql language (2010), https://prism.ucalgary.ca/handle/1880/104364
17. Rizvi, S., Mendelzon, A.O., Sudarshan, S., Roy, P.: Extending query rewriting techniques for fine-grained access control. In: SIGMOD Conference, pp. 551–562. ACM, France (2004)
18. Rogers, J., Bater, J., He, X., Machanavajjhala, A., Suresh, M., Wang, X.: Privacy changes everything. In: Gadepally, V., et al. (eds.) DMAH/Poly -2019. LNCS, vol. 11721, pp. 96–111. Springer, Cham (2019). https://doi.org/10.1007/978-3-030-33752-0_7
19. Schwarzkopf, M., Kohler, E., Frans Kaashoek, M., Morris, R.: Position: GDPR compliance by construction. In: Gadepally, V., et al. (eds.) DMAH/Poly -2019. LNCS, vol. 11721, pp. 39–53. Springer, Cham (2019). https://doi.org/10.1007/978-3-030-33752-0_3
20. Shastri, S., Banakar, V., Wasserman, M., Kumar, A., Chidambaram, V.: Understanding and benchmarking the impact of GDPR on database systems. Proc. VLDB Endow. **13**(7), 1064–1077 (2020)
21. Spenger, J., Carbone, P., Haller, P.: Wip: pods: privacy compliant scalable decentralized data services. PVLDB **12921**(1), 70–82 (2021)
22. Tsai, L., Schwarzkopf, M., Kohler, E.: Privacy heroes need data disguises. In: Proceedings of the Workshop on Hot Topics in Operating Systems, pp. 112–118. Association for Computing Machinery, Michigan (2021)
23. Wang, L., et al.: Data capsule: a new paradigm for automatic compliance with data privacy regulations, pp. 3–23. CoRR abs/1909.00077 (2019)

DMAH 2022

Enabling Real-World Medicine with Data Lake Federation: A Research Perspective

Cinzia Cappiello$^{(\boxtimes)}$, Marco Gribaudo, Pierluigi Plebani, Mattia Salnitri, and Letizia Tanca

Politecnico di Milano, Piazza Leonardo da Vinci 32, 20133 Milano, Italy
{cinzia.cappiello,marco.gribaudo,pierluigi.plebani,
mattia.salnitri,letizia.tanca}@polimi.it

Abstract. The collection of data during the routine delivery of care is changing the healthcare sector. Indeed, only from the clinical trial data it is difficult to obtain such a complete picture of the status of a patient as that provided by real-world data. However, the creation of valuable real-word evidence requires the adoption of an appropriate solution to ingest, store, and process the enormous amount of information coming from all the involved, typically heterogeneous data sources.

Data lake technologies are depicted as promising solutions for enhancing data management and analysis capabilities in the healthcare domain: we can rely on them to manage the complexity of big data volume and variety, providing data analysts with a self-service environment in which advanced analytics can be applied. In this paper we envision the adoption of a data lake federation through which organizations could achieve further benefits by sharing data. Exchanging data adds new research challenges related to guaranteeing data reliability and sovereignty. For instance, the collected data should be accurately described in order to document their quality, facilitate their discovery, define security and privacy policies. On the basis of the experience in Health Big Data, we are going to present an architecture for gathering real-world evidence, also identifying the research challenges from an IT perspective.

Keywords: Data lake federation · Data sharing · Data management

1 Introduction

In the recent years, Real World Evidence (RWE) is changing the way in which clinical trials are carried out, as the ever-increasing digitalization of the healthcare processes has enormously expanded the available amount of data related to the patients. Electronic Health Records (EHR), patient-monitoring data, data collected during previous clinical trials, just to name a few, contribute to the definition of real-world data, i.e., "the data relating to patient health status and/or to the delivery of health care routinely collected from a variety of sources" [20], that constitute the main pillar of real-world evidence.

E. K. Rezig et al. (Eds.): DMAH 2022/Poly 2022, LNCS 13814, pp. 39–56, 2022.
https://doi.org/10.1007/978-3-031-23905-2_4

From an organizational perspective, the adoption of a data-driven culture is required to exploit the full potential of the real world data that, on the one hand, extend the size as well as the formats of the data available, and on the other hand require appropriate support to the data governance to the end of increasing the quality of clinical trials. From a technological perspective, the platforms and technologies for Big Data Analytics, that have been proposed in the recent years for many domains, could be beneficial also in this scenario. However, the success of a data-driven culture is partially dependent on the ability to collect and analyze data gathered from multiple and heterogeneous sources [13], and the design of suitable data architectures plays a pivotal role. Many healthcare organizations rely on a data warehouse, but such a solution lacks the flexibility needed by the variety of required data analysis, and it is often not suitable to properly manage needs related to increasing volume and variety. New solutions are therefore needed, and the flexibility of the concept and technology of data lake is seen as promising for supporting the ever-growing requirements of data management and analysis capabilities. Data lakes are indeed fundamental to address the challenges of real-world evidence, since they constitute an effective tool to manage the power of big data technologies combining them with the agility of a self-service approach [10].

The goal of this paper is to propose an additional step in this direction of innovation, by proposing the adoption of an architecture for including the real world evidence based on a *data lake federation*, where local data architectures are connected in order to create a common data space in which data can be both used internally and easily shared. While this is a way to provide the organizations involved in clinical trials with the additional benefits offered by sharing data, at the same time, adopting and connecting data lakes in this complex scenario can be a challenging task, due to new privacy, infrastructural, and data management issues. This paper, on the basis of the experience in Health Big Data project[1], wants to report and discuss the advantages of the envisioned data lake federation, also highlighting the research challenges it proposes.

The rest of the paper is organized as follows. Section 2 provides a background to the discusses topic by referring to the relevant current literature. In Sect. 3, a motivating example adopted along the paper is introduced. Section 4 discusses the data lake federation as the architectural solution to boost the real-world medicine by simplifying data sharing. Section 5 introduces our idea of the most relevant research challenges of adopting a federated setting, and finally, Sect. 6 concludes the work by outlining the future directions.

2   Related Work

The core notion behind the concept of federated data lakes as opposed to distributed or decentralized ones lies in the interconnection and (loosely coupled) integration of independent and primarily self-contained data lakes controlled by different parties to achieve mutual benefits. Moving to a federation setting aims

---

[1] https://www.alleanzacontroilcancro.it/progetti/health-big-data/.

to solve the limitation of centralized approaches which led to a failure due to the complexity generated by the diverse data sources and the lack of flexibility when the data lake relies on a single technology [21]. At the same time, since the federation involves different and independent organizations data sovereignty [9] must be preserved and this is particularly relevant in the health domain where most of the considered data can be classified as sensitive data, thus subject to strict norms and rules (e.g., GDPR).

In this context, technical approaches to establishing trust in federated data management therefore necessarily include measures that makes doubtlessly determinable how the data sharing occurs and if the agreement is respected. Respective challenges have been subject to research in the past (with proposed solutions ranging from centralized approval gateways to remote auditing [18] and trusted logging/auditing mechanisms [16]), but primarily followed rather centralized or bilateral, inherently hierarchical approaches.

Moreover, when data are distributed and (partially) replicated across different entities, as in case of the nodes of the federation, ensuring consistency between these entities is a necessary precondition. While distributed database technologies has focused on ensuring consistency also for NoSQL based solutions [4], more recently, blockchains and distributed ledger technologies extended the addressed consistency challenges beyond merely technical decentralization towards decentralized control/ownership.

Based on this background, this paper investigates the adoption of a data lake federation in the health domain, which poses specific challenges related to the involved data types, formats, and size.

3   Case Study

To better guide the reader in the discussion about the research challenges in supporting RWE with a federated setting, we will refer to a case study inspired by a real scenario currently investigated in the Health Big Data (HBD) project[2].

More specifically, the considered clinical trial concerns an Italian hospital (called for simplicity ACME Hospital) that wants to study if the Next Generation Sequencing (NGS) is reliable when looking for markers of lung cancer in patients' genomes (see Fig. 1). To this aim, the ACME Hospital needs to find patients in Italy who are suffering from this specific disease and are associated with digital records in which the tumor marker is reported. Collecting these data, the Hospital aims to create a golden dataset including a set of patients characterized by the tumor markers that have been found.

Having these data, the final objective of the trial is to contact as many patients as possible and ask them to undergo a biopsy. Applying the NGS process to the collected organic material, the ACME Hospital wants to check whether

---

[2] For privacy purposes it is not possible at this stage to give additional information about the case study, such as, for instance, the actors involved or details on the considered population.

the NGS can find the same tumor marker(s) that had already been found in the past with traditional approaches, as reported in the golden set.

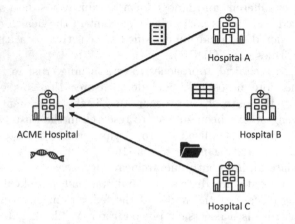

Fig. 1. NGS validation in lung cancer.

According to this scenario, the main problems that the ACME Hospital is facing is to reduce the burden of collecting these data, since the required information is dispersed among different nodes, managed by different systems, and stored in different formats. In each single involved hospital, the information about the patients is recorded in different ways and formats, which depend on the technology adopted for the storage. Data about patients can be retrieved from their Electronic Health Records (EHR), if present; in addition, for the patients who have been previously involved in a trial, other data about them could be found in a Clinical Trial Management Systems (CTMS). Finally, as usually happens, ad-hoc files (e.g., Excel files), are locally used by the different labs to store more information.

In this situation, the problem is not only related to *where* the data can be found, but also on *how* to find them. Currently, the only possible way to get this information entails a highly inefficient approach that necessarily involves personal and physical connection with the people in charge of the related data in the respective hospitals. In the lucky case that all these people are aware of the position of all the data stored in their hospitals, authorization processes must be finalized to have the right to access to them.

Finally, even in case this information can be obtained, a lot of effort is required to harmonize and integrate them in a way that allows the ACME Hospital to create the golden set to which the results of the NGS processing should be compared.

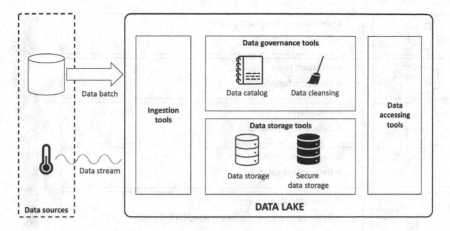

Fig. 2. Data lake minimal architecture

4 Data Lake Federation

By the term data lake (a.k.a. data lakehouse) we commonly refer to a platform composed of a set of software tools supporting the acquisition, the governance, and the provisioning of heterogeneous datasets to improve the effectiveness and the efficiency of data analytics, especially when considering the Big Data domain. Due to their flexibility in managing both structured and non structured data, and the possibility to customize the way in which the data are accessed, data lake solutions are preferable to the classical approached based on data warehouses. Indeed, data lakes do not require to organize the managed data in multidimensional schemas (e.g., hypercubes), but data are usually stored in their native formats, leaving the appropriate transformation to the final users, e.g., the data scientists. Conversely, data governance is more focused on data curation to increase the quality - and thus the value - of the data. As shown in Fig. 2, a basic data lake architecture is composed of:

- Tools for data ingestion to load data from the data sources, depending on the nature of the source, in a batch or stream mode.
- Tools for data governance that, among the others, include those for data curation and the data catalog.
- Tools for data storage, which also include specific solutions for storing sensitive data.
- Tools for data access, to enable the final users – such as business analysts or data scientists – to search and obtain the data they desire.

To implement such a federation, the proposed approach is inspired by the layers defined in a Service Oriented Architecture [19], re-elaborated as shown in Fig. 3. Generally speaking, the architecture combines the perspective of each node (i.e., local organization), in charge of the lower layers, and the perspective of the federation, covered by the upper layers.

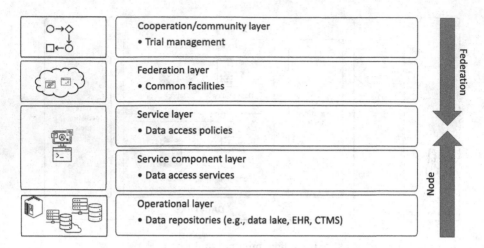

Fig. 3. Data lake federation reference architecture

The *operational layer* includes the facilities hosted and managed by the nodes of the federation to manage data which can be considered under the umbrella of the real world data and that could be potentially shared with other nodes. In the considered domain, we assume that health-related organizations (e.g., hospitals, research centres, pharmaceuticals) have implemented their own data repositories (data lakes or other) to store the data about patients, exams, treatments, trials, and many other kinds of information. While a single data lake offers services for dealing with the locally-stored data, the research based on real-world evidence can take advantage of a fruitful data sharing among all the organizations, which can be obtained by a federation of data lakes. From an infrastructural perspective, such facilities might be deployed either on the organization's premises or on cloud resources, and it might also be possible that some of them be deployed using a hybrid solution – based on the computing continuum paradigm [2] – which combines both resources on-premise and on cloud.

Assuming that each node decides which are the datasets to be made externally available (and under which constraints), the *service component layer* concerns the implementation of the data-access services, in charge to expose the selected datasets. For each service, depending on the nature of the data and the type of support that the node wants to offer, e.g., a simple FTP connection, a REST API. As the accessing methods may differ in terms of level of automation, this could contribute in different ways to the creation of a seamless integrated federation. It is worth noticing that, as the goal is the create a federation, the offered services could be not only limited to the data. In fact, each node – depending the available resources – could also offer to the other nodes of the federation additional services: from infrastructural (e.g., storage), to application (e.g., software for data analysis) resources.

The *service layer* completes the description of the data access services with the formalization of the policies that regulate the access to the exposed datasets through the defined services. Depending on the nature of the data, as well as the potential users, the policies specify who has the right to access what, and also which type of analysis can be performed on a given dataset or which are the transformations that must be applied to a dataset (e.g., anonymization) before making it available to the requester. Similarly, in case the node offers other resources than data, the access policies to these resources are defined as well.

Assuming that a set of nodes offers data services according to the structure just described, the envisioned data lake federation has the role to create an ecosystem that enables data sharing. To this aim, the *federation layer* offers both infrastructural and application services. For instance, a community cloud can be established to offer common storage and computation facilities that can be used by the node to (temporarily) store data in a convenient place to increase the performance. At the same time, a distributed monitoring system can be offered, to check if the occurring data-sharing is respecting the defined access policies. Finally, to support the goal of the federation, the upper layer offers the tools to define and manage *multi-centric clinical trials*, i.e., where the analysed data could be stored in more than one node.

5   Research Challenges

The design and implementation of the data lake federation described in Sect. 4 raise several challenges related to ensuring efficient and appropriate data storage, management and access. In details, for a single node involved in the envisioned ecosystem, the design of a data lake requires to define (i) a suitable infrastructure for a fast and controlled ingestion of data and subsequent storage; (ii) models and tools to support data reconciliation and integration; (iii) a data catalogue for describing sources in such a way as to facilitate their search, exploration, and integration; (iv) the way in which security and privacy requirements should be managed. In the following, the most relevant research challenges concerning the realization of a federated data lake system are discussed.

5.1   Infrastructure

A high-level view of the infrastructure for supporting the considered scenario is shown in Fig. 4. Computational and storage resources are divided into resources available in each node, and cloud-based services. Computational resources require both CPU and GPU support, while the storage is organized into a *Hot Storage* that contains data requiring quick access, and a cheaper, but slower *Cold Storage* aimed at maintaining less frequently used data. Data analysis can be performed both on-premises and on the cloud; for simplicity, we suppose that queries will be always originated from a cloud-based applications, allowing the users to exploit their own personal devices. The network is used both when transferring data to the cloud (the *Ingestion phase*), and during the querying process: however, the former requires resources that are generally several orders of magnitude larger than the latter.

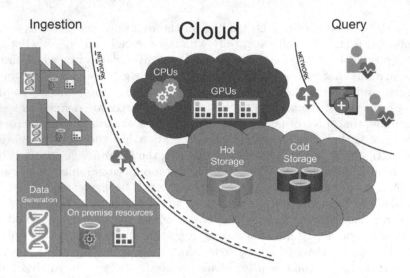

Fig. 4. The considered infrastructure.

In this scenario, the two most challenging infrastructural tasks are:

How Should Raw Data be Stored and Handled?

Each trial can produce a different amount of data depending on their nature: text-based reports (10^3B), RX images (10^7B), CT scans (10^9B) and genome sequencing (10^{11}B). For the largest types, the ingestion phase becomes a real challenge, and the network becomes the real limiting factor for transferring raw data to the cloud. Each raw data element follows the life cycle depicted in Fig. 5. Immediately after the ingestion a filtering stage extracts a first set of metadata (called *Pre-filtering* in the picture), but further analysis in future studies can also be performed (*Re-filtering*). Filtering is usually very resource demanding from both a computational and I/O point of view: depending on the scenario, it might occur either on local premises, or on the cloud. Then, after a time period that spans from few months to a few years depending on the context, the raw data become less likely to be need, and it can be transferred to a cold storage for cost reduction[3]. In some cases, these raw data might be needed again, thus requiring it to return to the hot storage and undergo new filtering stages. Finally, after a time period in the range of tens of years, data become obsolete, and they might be deleted.

How can Computational Resources be Managed?

The biggest challenge for managing the computational resources comes from the heterogeneity of the tools commonly used to filter raw-data. Trials, belonging to a large variety of contexts, require totally different tools, exploiting different resources. In particular, some need a large amount of memory, others very fast

---

[3] For simplicity, we can suppose that cold storage will be based on the cloud.

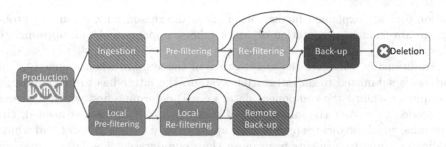

Fig. 5. The life-cycle of raw data.

storage access, or the availability of a sufficiently large number of GPUs. Forcing all the users to rely on a single technology (i.e., a Linux VM in a IaaS deployment) might be too limiting, but allowing too many services (i.e., Hadoop and Spark clusters, Docker based conainers as well as IaaS VMs) might prevent the possibility of supporting a real data integration.

5.2   Data Integration

Data integration is the problem of combining data residing at different sources, and providing the user with a unified view of this data [14]. The problem of designing data integration systems is important in current real-world applications, and is characterized by a number of difficult issues; however, in the specific case of health-related data for experiments, the main challenges related to integration are the need to put together all the data related to a specific patient, and the need to compare data of any kind (e.g., images, sequences, time series, medical reports...) to the end of deriving their similarities and differences.

Traditionally, data integration system can be classified into two large categories: (i) the data sources contain the real data, while a global schema provides a virtual, integrated view of the underlying sources; and (ii) the data of the data sources are integrated and stored into another appropriate system, as in the case of data warehouses. In both cases, the integration system is in charge of providing a reconciled, integrated view of the underlying sources, that in case (i) is actually virtual since the physical data still reside in the data sources in their original form.

Recently, in view of the enormous amount and variety of resources available in the organizations and on the Internet, this paradigm has been relaxed, giving rise to much looser integration schemes, such as *data spaces* [5] and their concrete implementations, the data lakes.

As already mentioned, however, data lakes are not (only) a data integration tool, but their goal is to provide some basic operations, like keyword search over its data sources, and, possibly, also more sophisticated ones like relational-style queries, data mining, or monitoring over certain sources. In this case, additional services can be provided, to support integration in the so-called *pay-as-you-go* fashion, quickly explained further on. This is the reason why, given the problem we are facing, a (federation of) data lake(s) appears to be an appropriate solution.

Traditionally, whatever the architecture of the system, when a query, or an update, is submitted to an integration system, the latter has to decompose it into queries against the component data, i.e.: (i) determine first which datasets are needed to answer the query, and, if more than one dataset is needed, (ii) determine which predicates (conditions) apply to only a single dataset and which predicates apply to elements from more than one dataset. The latter ones can only be evaluated over all the involved datasets, appropriately combined, whereas each of the former can be evaluated over the specific dataset addressed by that (sub)query. Therefore, whatever the supporting technology, query processing in data integration requires some reformulation steps: the initial query, addressed to the integration system, has to be reformulated in terms of a set of queries over the single datasets.

In a data lake, these operations are performed in a pay-as-you-go fashion, avoiding the creation of mediated schemas or the permanent establishment of relationships between the elements of two different sources (entity resolution and data fusion), and relying instead on temporary links based on accurate descriptions of the data by means of metadata (see Sect. 5.3). Basically, the data lake offers a system that provides useful services on a collection of heterogeneous data with very little up-front effort. The basic tools for doing this are:

- keyword search over a collection of data coupled with effective data visualization. This can be enriched with some of the techniques for automatic, on-the-fly matching of schemata or instances, and automatic extraction of metadata.
- improving the metadata in the system to the end of supporting and validating schema mappings, instance and reference reconciliation, or improve the results of information extraction.

The individual data sources that participate in a data lake can be relational databases, XML or text datasets, images, time series, or even web services, therefore some of them might support actual query languages and others offer a simple keyword-based query facility. Consider now the two integration challenges we listed before.

How do We Put Together All the Data Related to a Specific Patient?
This task appears to be rather trivial, since nowadays all people's data can be easily identified by means of some kind of personal code like the SSN, and this can be used to collect each patient's data together. And in fact, the second one is the real challenge:

How do We Compare Data of Any Kind (e.g., Images, Time Series, Medical Reports...) to the End of Deriving Their Similarities and Differences?
The integration of natural language text can be supported by semantic techniques that may be based on ontologies (very numerous and rich in the health

domain) and/or on ML tools, such as word and sentence embeddings. Queries that require to retrieve images, or time series, that show some resemblance, might be based on keyword-search on the image features or other metadata, but might also exploit some service based on image or plot similarity. The data lake should "know", or be able to establish, a relationship between datasets that have different characteristics, and also allow different modes of interaction, offering appropriate services to different types of content. For this, it is fundamental to maintain a catalog of descriptive metadata about the data lake contents, from the most basic, such as source name, location, size, creation date and owner, to the most sophisticated ones, like image or movie features. This information is the basis to allow search and query over all the contents of the data lake, regardless of their formats. Moreover, the data lake should also support data updates, also based on the same search techniques.

5.3   Data Cataloguing

The users of a data lake are various: they can range from experts, who are accustomed to deal with data cleaning and analysis techniques, to less experienced users who need support to search and extract data. For this reason, the data catalog plays a fundamental role in the data lake design. It has to organize and describe data in a way to ease data access, exploration and discovery.

In fact, it is often difficult to understand the contents of a raw dataset. Field names are hard to understand, and in some datasets (e.g., unstructured sources) the schema specification is completely missing. Even when field names are well specified they might be not consistent among different datasets, hindering data mapping and integration. For this reason, in order to align datasets, a manual inspection would be the best solution, but this is not feasible with the volume and variety of datasets that characterize a data lake [10].

Data catalogs offer a solution, annotating datasets with consistent business terms and providing interfaces that allow users to search for data using a well-known vocabulary. Data catalogs should contain information about the content, quality, provenance, and trustworthiness of the datasets.

The design of data catalogs in the considered scenario raise the following research challenges.

Which are the Relevant Metadata to be Included in the Data Catalog?
The identification of all the relevant metadata to consider for the description of the sources is not a simple task. Data lakes have been defined to be flexible, so that users with different skills and experience can access data to perform the tasks they need. Users' requirements are various and unknown, and the catalog has to describe the data sources in a comprehensive way in order to allow different analyses and to satisfy different needs.

In the literature, data catalogs usually contain two main categories of metadata: technical and business metadata. *Technical metadata* are related to the profile of the datasets (e.g., list of attributes, data types, statical information). *Business metadata* provide a business description of a dataset. Most metadata of the former class can be retrieved automatically by using appropriate data profiling tools. While the latter usually require referring to ontologies or folksnomies. In order to support data sharing among the different nodes of the data lake federation additional metadata should be considered. First of all data sharing requires trust among the parties and this can be reached by enriching the description of the data sources with information related to data quality and data provenance. The data quality level of a dataset can be described by using the traditional data quality dimensions (e.g., completeness, consistency) and additional properties able to reveal the presence of errors or biases. However, defining a data quality model is not simple when the sources are heterogeneous. In fact, the literature provides the definition of data quality dimensions for structured databases while for other sources, which are commonly used in the healthcare domain (e.g., text, images) a consolidated set of data quality properties is missing. Data provenance needs to describe all the operations performed on the dataset including responsibilities (i.e., who did what) and temporal details. This also allow data scientists to understand if data are reliable.

Always with the aim of supporting the discovery and use of datasets, metadata to support data integration are needed. For this reason, for example, information related to data interdependencies, relationships among attributes of different schemas, and overlaps between datasets is needed.

Finally, datasets should be described also from the security and privacy point of view in order to guarantee that data are treated according to the right policies and regulations. This is important both for an internal use of data but also in the data sharing perspective.

How Should the Tagging Process be Designed?
Tagging refers to the process with which metadata are assigned to the datasets. In general, this can be performed manually or automatically. Considering the data volume that characterizes a data lake we can state that a complete manual process is not practical since it is extremely time consuming. New tools for the automatic tagging are available but a completely automatic approach can introduce some errors. A viable option is the adoption of a mixed strategy in which automatic tools are used with a Human In the Loop approach. The user can check the tags defined by the tool and reject or substitute the ones that are not correct [10].

5.4   Data Movement

In addition to the possibility to share data, a data lake federation also offers a valuable environment to share computation. This increases the number of possible configurations with which the data analytics can be performed, by balancing between data and computation movement [3].

In the considered domain, clinical trials could require the analysis of datasets of different sizes and complexities, and moreover the computation can be heavy or light depending on the types of analysis. For instance, the ACME Hospital needs to analyse genomes and to compare the results with more synthetic data, i.e., the list of tumor markers. In this case, it is reasonable to assume that the ACME Hospital has enough resources to generate, analyse, and host the result of the sequencing. Yet, the size of the list of tumor markers observed in the patients of the other hospitals can be sent to the ACME Hospital with no impact on the performance.

But, what if the biopsy and the related genomes are sequenced directly at the other hospitals? Is it reasonable to transmit the genomes to the ACME Hospital to compare the information about the tumor marker or is it more convenient to perform also the comparison at the hospital premises? These questions are two possible examples of how different settings can be possible when a data lake federation exists, assuming that the belonging nodes also agree on the possibility to execute some pieces of code on behalf of other nodes. Based on these considerations, the following three research challenges are defined.

Which are the Attributes of the Datasets and the Characteristics of the Analysis that Contribute to Decide Whether to Move the Data or the Computation?

Closely related to the metadata identification required for building a data catalog, as discussed in Sect. 5.3, especially the technical metadata can help – and they might be extended – to decide whether to move data or computation. For instance, the size of the dataset or the quality of network connection could suggest to leave the data where they are stored, as the time needed to transfer the data could negatively impact the overall performance. In this case, the alternative is to enact the data sharing by allowing the actor that needs those data to perform the computation remotely. Actually, these metadata concerning the dataset covers only half of the story: metadata about the computation must be also considered to understand which are the peculiarities of the analysis that should be performed on the data. Here the challenge is to identify a common and sufficient set of computation-related metadata, which can be used to understand if the analysis can be executed remotely. If, on the one side, container-based solutions (e.g., docker, podman) improve the code mobility, on the other side hosting nodes have to satisfy a minimal set of system requirements. To this aim, the data lakes in the federation should include also a service catalog, in which these metadata are used to classify the software tools for data analytics.

How is it Possible to Securely Host Data and Run Code in a Mode on Behalf of other Nodes?

The possibility to allow moving not only the data but also the code, if one the one side is beneficial in terms of privacy issues (e.g., the data do not move away from the node, but only the result of the analysis), on the other side the trust on the data sharing strictly depends on the trust of the software that the node has to host. The challenge is to offer trusted security environment, which is able to run the hosted code without the risk that this code could affect the rest of the system and by ensuring that it has visibility only on the data that have been agreed to be shared. Standardized approaches are thus required to maintain a certain level of interoperability, to avoid the risk that this type of data sharing configuration could be denied.

How is it Possible to Track the Way in Which Shared Data and Applications to be Sure that the Nodes Behave Correctly?
Regardless of whether the data or the computation are moving, if data are moved from Hospital A to ACME Hospital, the former does loose the control on the data. ACME Hospital, once getting the copy, can potentially operate on the data also for other reasons than the one agreed. Conversely, if the ACME Hospital decides to deploy the code of the analysis to the Hospital A premises, the former does loose the control on the computation and the sandbox in which it will be deployed could alter the results before it is sent back. As a consequence, it is fundamental to create a trust environment, which is able to both track and possible enforce, the agreement between the parties. In this context, solutions based on containerized data able to control – and if needed limiting – the access, blockchain-based solution could be beneficial. At the same time, this requires to define standard formats for exposing data and logging the data access which could hamper the joining to the federation.

5.5   Data Privacy

Privacy is a key concept and requirement in federated data lakes. Being deployed in the European Economic Area (EEA) and using data of European citizens, the data lake federation proposed in this paper must follow the European General Data Protection Regulation (GDPR) [8,17]. The architecture we propose will also store data of citizens of countries outside of the EEA, that are protected with other privacy laws, however, this paper focuses on the protection of EEA citizens, in particular the Italian citizens, leaving the implementation of other privacy laws for future work.

The adoption of a data lake federation opens the possibility to create a trusted environment based on shared policy models which can be used to express, monitor, and enforce privacy requirements. To this aim, some challenges need to be considered as discussed in the next paragraphs.

Which Data, Stored and Shared in the Architecture, Must be Protected?
GDPR categorizes data in three types:

- anonymous data: data that *do not contain* information that can be used to identify a person;
- personal data: data that *contain* information that can be used to identify a person;
- sensitive data: personal data that contain information on physical, mental health or condition and other particular conditions. For the full list of sensitive data please refer to [8].

GDPR protects personal data, including sensitive data. For the latter, a higher lever of security is required by the law. Health-care datasets that are stored and shared by the architecture are sensitive data. The data lake federation, consequently, will have to deploy all the required privacy and security measures defined by the European law.

Clinical trials can be categorised in *prospective*, if they use data that will be collected for the experiment, or *retrospective* if they use data that were collected for other trials and are already present in the database.

Following this categorization, the federated data lake will host data for *secondary uses* of *retrospective* clinical trials. As a matter of fact, the architecture will store datasets collected by other experiments (secondary usage of data gathered for other purposes) and it will make them available for clinical trials that will base their analysis in already existing data (retrospective trials). For example, the ACME Hospital, described in Sect. 3, gathers information of patients already (retrospective trial) collected for other trials (secondary purpose). It may also store data of prospective clinical trials: in this case the datasets are fed incrementally while the trials are taking place.

It is worth noticing that personal, and sensitive, data are not the only types of data that need be protected. Other types of data are relevant assets for health organizations, for example the results of the clinical trials. However, this Section focuses on data that are protected by the GDPR, whose protection is central, since an eventual loss of these data will cause: (i) a loss of trust of the patients of the structure; (ii) a relevant monetary loss, since the GDPR imposes fines "of up to 20 million euros, or, in the case of an undertaking, up to 4% of its entire global turnover of the preceding fiscal year, whichever is higher" [8]; (iii) auditing and legal issues for the organization.

Which Legal Basis can be Used for Sharing Health Care Data?
GDPR allows sharing personal and sensitive data for the following lawful basis: consent, performance of a contract, a legitimate interest, a vital interest, a legal requirement, and a public interest. Consent is the most known and used, yet, it cannot be adopted for the federated data lakes. The consent, as it is defined in the GDPR, must state the specific purposes of the project that uses the personal data, while the architecture proposed in this paper has the objective of sharing data among health care organizations, making it impossible to foresee all possible purposes of the trials that will use the shared datasets. Unfortunately, this is valid for both retrospective and prospective trials: for the former, consents are collected when data are collected and cannot be modified making it impossible to add the purpose of the new trial; for the latter, the specificity of the consent does not allow to use general terms or make it open for other, unknown, trials. This is required since prospective trials create datasets that will be used by retrospective trials. Moreover, for retrospective trials, in many case patients may not be able to sign new consents because of the illness they are affected or because the may be deceased.

Due to these reasons, the architecture adopts as lawful base the public interest and, in particular, what is described in the Article 9(2)(j) of the GDPR for research purposes.

Which Mechanisms Should be Used to Protect Health Care Data?
The specification on the security mechanisms to be used for the protection of sensitive data is contained in the GDPR - partially -, and in local privacy laws (the architecture described in this paper will be deploy and share data in Italy and, therefore, it will implement the Italian laws such as the 101/2018 [1]). The federated data lake architecture will be stored in nodes certificated with security standards ISO\IEC 27001 [11] and ISO\IEC 27018 [12]. This will guarantee a level of security compliant with the GDPR.

As introduced in the beginning of this section on privacy challenges, only personal data need be protected. Another frequently adopted strategy consists in stripping personal identificators from personal data: this operation will generate anonymous data that are not protected by privacy laws and can be freely shared. Unluckily, anonymization removes information, and thus lowers the data utility, removing, for example, the link between different exams of the same patient [15]. For some analyses, anonymous data can be enough but not for all of them, making the storage of personal data in the architecture necessary.

It is worth noticing that, even if anonymous and pseudo-anonymous data are not protected by the GDPR and privacy laws, they are still an asset of health organizations and need to be protected as well.

6   Concluding Remarks

With the aim of defining an architecture that exploits the full potential of real world data to increase the effectiveness and efficacy of data analytics in healthcare, this paper has presented a solution based on a data lake federation. Being a first attempt in this direction, the paper shares the set of research challenges that the studies conducted so far have found relevant. The main challenges concern the infrastructure, how data can be integrated, data cataloguing, data movement and privacy. With this paper, the authors want to stimulate the community to deal with the identified research challenges, to improve the possibility to easily share healthcare data among medical research centers and organizations, removing data sharing hindrances that too frequently pose barriers for clinical trials.

As a natural continuation in this study, the focus will be to provide methods and tools to solve the identified research challenges. In particular, an important aspect that will be considered will concern the compliance with the norms and rules that, at least at the European level, are emerging, e.g., the Data Governance Act [6] and Data Act [7]. In fact, building a solution on common and shared background will facilitate the adoption of the envisioned data lake federation.

Acknowledgment. This work has been partially supported by the Health Big Data Project (CCR-2018-23669122), funded by the Italian Ministry of Economy and Finance and coordinated by the Italian Ministry of Health and the network Alleanza Contro il Cancro.

References

1. Decreto Legislativo 196/2003, integrated with D.lgs 101/2018. Gazzetta ufficiale (2018)
2. Bermbach, D., et al.: A research perspective on fog computing. In: Braubach, L., et al. (eds.) ICSOC 2017. LNCS, vol. 10797, pp. 198–210. Springer, Cham (2018). https://doi.org/10.1007/978-3-319-91764-1_16
3. Cappiello, C., et al.: Improving health monitoring with adaptive data movement in fog computing. Front. Robot. AI **7** (2020). https://doi.org/10.3389/frobt.2020.00096, https://www.frontiersin.org/article/10.3389/frobt.2020.00096
4. Diogo, M., Cabral, B., Bernardino, J.: Consistency models of nosql databases. Futur. Internet **11**(2) (2019). https://doi.org/10.3390/fi11020043, https://www.mdpi.com/1999-5903/11/2/43
5. Doan, A., Halevy, A.Y., Ives, Z.G.: Principles of Data Integration. Morgan Kaufmann, Burlington (2012). http://research.cs.wisc.edu/dibook/
6. European Commission: Regulation of the european parliament and of the council on european data governance (data governance act), November 2020. https://eur-lex.europa.eu/legal-content/EN/TXT/?uri=CELEX:52020PC0767
7. European Commission: Regulation of the European parliament and of the council on Harmonised rules on fair access to and use of data (data act), February 2022. https://eur-lex.europa.eu/legal-content/EN/ALL/?uri=CELEX:52022PC0068
8. European Parliament and Council of the European Union: Regulation (EU) 2016/679 of the European Parliament and of the Council of 27 April 2016 on the protection of natural persons with regard to the processing of personal data and on the free movement of such data, and repealing Directive 95/46/EC (General Data Protection Regulation). Official Journal of the European Union (2016)
9. Geisler, S., et al.: Knowledge-driven data ecosystems toward data transparency. ACM J. Data Inf. Qual. **14**(1), 3:1–3:12 (2022). https://doi.org/10.1145/3467022
10. Gorelik, A.: The Enteprise Big Data Lake. O' Reilly, Sebastopol (2019)
11. ISO Central Secretary: Information security management. Standard ISO/IEC 27001, International Organization for Standardization, Geneva, CH (2018). https://www.iso.org/isoiec-27001-information-security.html
12. ISO Central Secretary: Information technology - security techniques - code of practice for protection of personally identifiable information (pii) in public clouds acting as pii processors. Standard ISO/IEC 27018, International Organization for Standardization, Geneva, CH (2019). https://www.iso.org/standard/76559.html
13. Kondylakis, H., Koumakis, L., Tsiknakis, M., Marias, K.: Implementing a data management infrastructure for big healthcare data. In: 2018 IEEE EMBS International Conference on Biomedical Health Informatics (BHI), pp. 361–364 (2018). https://doi.org/10.1109/BHI.2018.8333443
14. Lenzerini, M.: Data integration: a theoretical perspective. In: Popa, L., Abiteboul, S., Kolaitis, P.G. (eds.) Proceedings of the Twenty-first ACM SIGACT-SIGMOD-SIGART Symposium on Principles of Database Systems, 3–5 June, Madison, Wisconsin, USA, pp. 233–246. ACM (2002). https://doi.org/10.1145/543613.543644
15. Li, T., Li, N.: On the tradeoff between privacy and utility in data publishing. In: Proceedings of the 15th ACM SIGKDD International Conference on Knowledge Discovery and Data Mining, pp. 517–526 (2009)
16. Lins, S., Schneider, S., Sunyaev, A.: Trust is good, control is better: creating secure clouds by continuous auditing. IEEE Trans. Cloud Comput. **6**(3), 890–903 (2018). https://doi.org/10.1109/TCC.2016.2522411

17. Salnitri, M., Jürjens, J., Mouratidis, H., Mancini, L., Giorgini, P. (eds.): Visual Privacy Management. LNCS, vol. 12030. Springer, Cham (2020). https://doi.org/10.1007/978-3-030-59944-7
18. Sookhak, M., et al.: Remote data auditing in cloud computing environments: a survey, taxonomy, and open issues. ACM Comput. Surv. **47**(4) (2015). https://doi.org/10.1145/2764465
19. The Open Group: Soa reference architecture. https://www.opengroup.org/soa/source-book/soa_refarch/index.htm
20. U.S. Food and Drug Administration: Framework for fda's real-word evidence program, December 2018. https://www.fda.gov/media/120060/download
21. Dehghani, Z.: How to move beyond a monolithic data lake to a distributed data mesh, May 2019. https://martinfowler.com/articles/data-monolith-to-mesh.html

Towards Assessing Data Bias in Clinical Trials

Chiara Criscuolo$^{(\boxtimes)}$, Tommaso Dolci, and Mattia Salnitri

Politecnico di Milano, Piazza Leonardo da Vinci, 32, 20133 Milan, Italy
{chiara.criscuolo,tommaso.dolci,mattia.salnitri}@polimi.it

Abstract. Algorithms and technologies are essential tools that pervade all aspects of our daily lives. In the last decades, health care research benefited from new computer-based recruiting methods, the use of federated architectures for data storage, the introduction of innovative analyses of datasets, and so on. Nevertheless, health care datasets can still be affected by data bias. Due to data bias, they provide a distorted view of reality, leading to wrong analysis results and, consequently, decisions. For example, in a clinical trial that studied the risk of cardiovascular diseases, predictions were wrong due to the lack of data on ethnic minorities. It is, therefore, of paramount importance for researchers to acknowledge data bias that may be present in the datasets they use, eventually adopt techniques to mitigate them and control if and how analyses results are impacted.

This paper proposes a method to address bias in datasets that: *(i)* defines the types of data bias that may be present in the dataset, *(ii)* characterizes and quantifies data bias with adequate metrics, *(iii)* provides guidelines to identify, measure, and mitigate data bias for different data sources. The method we propose is applicable both for prospective and retrospective clinical trials. We evaluate our proposal both through theoretical considerations and through interviews with researchers in the health care environment.

Keywords: Data bias · Health care · Data management

1 Introduction

In the last decades evidence-based medicine relied consistently on large datasets. New technologies, such as data mining and data lakes, allow to analyze larger and larger datasets obtaining astonishing results that led to new and more reliable therapies [8], such as in the case of diabetic retinopathy detection [16,22]. Yet, reliable results directly depend on high-quality datasets. Biased datasets, i.e., dataset that do not correctly represent the population, inevitably lead to distorted results. This is particularly important for evidence-based medicine, where wrong or not effective therapies might be applied as a consequence of wrong analyses. For instance, in the controversial case of IBM Watson Oncology

E. K. Rezig et al. (Eds.): DMAH 2022/Poly 2022, LNCS 13814, pp. 57–74, 2022.
https://doi.org/10.1007/978-3-031-23905-2_5

system, machine learning algorithms return erroneous recommendations whenever the training of the system is not well planned [15]. The identification and measurement of bias in health care dataset is, therefore, essential to have reliable results and high-quality health care.

Even though bias and its impacts are well studied in specific research fields and application sectors of Computer Science, such as automated-decision making for hiring [23], justice [2] or image recognition [29], they are not frequently considered for health care datasets. Unluckily, information on bias is not provided with these datasets, leaving researchers and doctors clueless on the possible impacts on their analysis and with no means to mitigate them [10]. In order to get the benefits of event-based medicine and, therefore, to provide the best possible health care, information bias need to be considered as an essential part of datasets. This issue affects both retrospective clinical trials, which use already collected datasets that may be affected by data bias unknown at the time of data collection, yet relevant for the current trial, and prospective clinical trials, where datasets are collected for a specific clinical experiment.

This paper provides an insightful definition of the types of data bias that may affect health care datasets for retrospective clinical trials, and a method that will help health care researchers in: (i) identifying and measuring bias for health care datasets; (ii) allowing them to filter datasets based on bias information that will be stored on metadata; (iii) choosing the appropriate mitigation action to reduce bias before using the dataset. This method can be used for perspective clinical trials by monitoring the data collection and guide researchers towards the mitigation of identified bias. To reach these objectives, this paper defines a set of guidelines that will guide researcher on the application of the method. The method proposed in this paper has been validated through interviews with health care researchers and experts in bioethics and philosophy.

The paper is structured as it follows. Section 2 gives an overview of the context of bias and health care datasets. Section 3 describes the baseline of this paper, while Sect. 4 provides the most relevant research work on data bias in health care datasets. Sections 5 and 6 are the contribution of this paper: they describe the method proposed, the types of data bias involved, measurements and mitigation actions. Section 7 illustrates the initial validation of the method proposed. Section 8 concludes the paper.

2   Data Bias in Health Care

Recently, in the context of health care research, the employment of new information technologies is steadily increasing, driven by the admirable goal of improving effectiveness and efficiency of various aspects of medicine. For instance, machine learning proved to be extremely effective when used for detecting diabetic retinopathy [16,22] and skin cancer [13], with results equal to or greater than those of human physicians. Combining big data and machine learning algorithms has been shown to significantly improve the accuracy of analyses [8].

However, despite the enormous advantages of using computer technologies in health care, serious ethical issues emerged on several occasions. For example, it has been shown that systems for algorithmic decision-making for medical diagnosis and treatment recommendations, despite improving accuracy, also increase opacity and uncertainty, especially when using deep learning techniques [15,36]. Opacity largely affects aspects such as accountability and fairness: famous is the case of IBM Watson Health, whose algorithms for cancer treatment recommendation turned out to be erroneous due to the small amount and the synthetic nature of the training data [15]. In this context, many of the emerged risks are related to data used to train the model or validate the underlying algorithms. In particular, the presence of bias in the data heightens the risk of unfairness and disparity. For instance, whenever a model is used for patients whose data differ from the data on which the model has been trained, results of the clinical trial are biased [31]. Also, bias may arise when the study population is not well selected [14].

In recent years, many ethical risks concern ethnic groups, which are often under-represented in clinical trials. Among the problems were the systematic misclassification of variants as pathogenic for Africans [25] and the inconsistent performance of risk calculators for cardiovascular disease in multi-ethnic studies, especially for ethnic minorities such as African Caribbeans and South Asian women [35]. Additionally, new frontiers of medicine such as genome sequencing tend to exclude ethnic minorities in a worrying way, as evident from the fact that by 2009 fewer than one percent of genome investigations included Africans [39].

3   Preliminaries

Considerable research attention is being paid to aspects of responsible data analysis and *Data Science Ethics*, which lays the foundation for data bias analysis. Data Science Ethics highlights the need for ethical analyses, focusing on concepts such as fairness, diversity, accountability, transparency and privacy. It analyzes the meaning and nature of computational operations, the interactions between hardware, software and data, considering the variety of digital technologies that make them possible. Data Science Ethics emphasizes the complexity of the ethical challenges posed by data science. The rest of this section gives definitions of fundamental concepts used in the rest of the paper: *Bias*, *Fairness* and *Diversity*.

Bias is defined as an "inclination, or prejudice for, or against one person, or group, especially in a way considered to be unfair" [30, p.4]. Sometimes bias is *desirable* and part of the correct system functionality. For example, in a system that predicts the likelihood of a person to have a specific disease, the group of individuals who actually has the disease should be systematically attributed a higher probability than the group who does not have it. An *undesired bias* is "a bias that is considered problematic, possibly unfair by the stakeholders of the system or other persons impacted by the system" [5, p.3]. Typically, this is observed when bias relates to a protected attribute, which is defined as "a sensitive attribute for which non-discrimination should be established" [38, p.2]. In the last few decades, many studies focused on the types of data bias that can be present in data [26,30].

Fairness, in the context of decision-making, is related to the concept of "absence of any prejudice or favoritism toward an individual or a group based on their inherent or acquired characteristics" [32, p.100]. It is also associated with the so-called "lack of bias" [33]. However, there is no universal definition of fairness, mainly because it is a broad concept that intersects different scenarios, thus in literature there are many formulations. To assess fairness there exist many formal metrics [38], such as statistical ones that evaluate the distribution of positive predictions among instances in the dataset.

Finally, **diversity** is "a general term used to capture the quality of a collection of items, or of a composite item, with regards to the variety of its constituent elements" [12, p.1]. There are many metrics to quantify diversity; some of them are based on the notion of distance and rely on pair-wise similarity between elements, while others are based on coverage, that measures the extent to which the elements cover a predefined number of aspects [12].

4   Related Work

In this section, we separate related work concerning methods for addressing data bias in generic datasets using Computer Science techniques, and, in the second part, methods that address data bias in health care.

4.1   Data Bias in Computer Science

Most of the works in Computer Science, and specifically in Data Science Ethics, focus on ensuring fairness, generally by algorithmic data bias discovery and mitigation in prediction tasks, more specifically for classification algorithms [1, 9,37].

There are three possible approaches to enforce fairness in data analysis applications: *(i) pre-processing techniques*, i.e., procedures to verify that the training data are fair before the application of the algorithm; *(ii) in-processing techniques*, i.e., procedures to ensure that, during the learning phase, the algorithm does not inherit the bias present in the data, and *(iii) post-processing techniques*, i.e., procedures to correct the algorithm predictions, and consequently decisions, and make them fairer.

In this context, one of the most notable work is *AI Fairness 360: An Extensible Toolkit for Detecting, Understanding, and Mitigating Unwanted Algorithmic Bias* [9], an open-source framework to reach algorithmic fairness for classifiers. AI Fairness 360 quantifies and mitigates data bias using a variety of statistical measures, exploiting pre-processing, in-processing and post-processing techniques.

A work that studies both fairness and diversity is *Nutritional Labels for Data and Models* by Stoyanovich and Howe [34]. The authors develop an interpretability and transparency tool based on the concept of *Nutritional Labels*, drawing an analogy to the food industry, where simple and standardized labels convey information about ingredients and production processes. *Ranking Facts* [34] is a system based on nutritional labels that visually expresses fairness through statistical measures, and diversity through the distribution for each category.

One more recent work is [3], a system to assess diversity, and more specifically coverage, for a given dataset over multiple categorical attributes. Based on new efficient techniques to identify the regions of the attribute space not adequately covered by data, this system can determine the least amount of data that must be added to solve the lack of diversity.

4.2 Data Bias in Health Care

In the area of health care, the majority of work focuses on theoretical and philosophical aspects, and only few of them give more precise guidelines about data bias identification and measurement.

A famous work is [11]: the authors analyze major challenges when implementing predictive analytics in health care settings. They make broad recommendations for overcoming challenges raised in the four phases of the lifecycle of a predictive analytics model: acquiring data to build the model, building and validating it, testing it in real-world settings, and disseminating and using it more broadly. According to the authors, it is essential for predictive analytics models to be constantly evaluated, updated, re-implemented, and reevaluated, because the presence of bias threatens the trust of patients, providers and the public. Nonetheless, the authors remain optimistic that predictive analytics can help build stronger and more dynamic systems.

Another notable work is [31], that presents a conceptual framework of how different types of bias relates to one another. From our point of view, it is particularly relevant the classification of bias that arise from machine learning algorithms in the health care area. The authors provide a list of data bias definitions divided into four categories: *bias in model design*, *bias in training data*, *bias in interactions with clinicians* and *bias in interactions with patients*. They also reveal that the interactions of model predictions with clinicians and patients may exacerbate health care disparities.

As far as we know, there is no method in literature that specifically guides the user in searching and measuring data bias in the health care context, using the instruments from Computer Science and particularly Data Science Ethics.

5 Method

We propose a framework that consists in a pipeline for identifying and measuring bias in health care datasets. This work targets health care researchers and provides a set of application guidelines to be used during clinical trials.

Our method answers to the following questions that health care researchers should have before adopting a health care dataset for clinical trials.

- Q1. Is there any data bias in the dataset?
- Q2. Which ones are they and how to measure them?
- Q3. How to reduce their impact?

Several actors will benefit from this method. First, health care researchers, who mainly exploit medical data to carry out clinical trials; they also represent the target users of our method. Secondly, physicians and patients, since they are directly or indirectly involved in the application of results from clinical trials, and in the usage of automated systems for medical diagnosis based on machine learning techniques. Finally, ethics committees will benefit from having guidelines to apply in the health care research context, to extend the ethical principles of medicine also to new, not yet widespread computer-based tools.

The data management pipeline defined in [5] delineates five main stages of the lifecycle of decision support systems: requirements, system design, construction, testing, and maintenance. The method we propose will be used after data have been extracted from health care datasets, at the beginning of the construction phase and before the analysis phase. This temporal position allows our method to be applied after data have been—at least partially—collected, but before the construction of the analysis algorithm. In fact, in our opinion, clinicians need to modify data before the beginning of the construction phase.

The method uses the data bias identified in [31] and described in Sect. 4, where a list of data bias in the context of health care are defined. The method we are proposing considers bias in training data, since bias in model design and related to clinicians and patients cannot be analyzed from a computer scientist perspective, due to the lack of measurement strategies. In particular, considered data bias are: *minority, missing data, informativeness* and *selection bias*.

5.1   Input/Output

The input of the method consists of a dataset and information on its application context. The method targets reasonably large datasets that are going to be used in machine learning analytics for evidence-based medicine. The output of the method consists of a list of biases that have been identified in the data source, their quantification through appropriate metrics, and possible mitigation actions to solve them. This output allows to: *(i)* inform the researcher about the level of fairness associated to the input dataset by using a variety of bias metrics; *(ii)* increase awareness about the limits of the outcome using the input dataset in clinical trials and consequently, the risks connected to its application; *(iii)* have adequate information for further uses of the datasets, that can be stored in metadata; *(iv)* choose a mitigation strategy that, by applying it, can produce a cleaned version of the input data source.

5.2   Steps

Figure 1 shows the pipeline of the method proposed in this paper. All steps, described below, will be executed by the health care researcher.

1. *Bias Identification* includes the study and analysis on the presence of different types of data bias.

2. *Bias Measurement*, where each data bias is mapped with its corresponding measurement techniques.
3. *Bias Mitigation*, where each data bias is associated to possible mitigation strategies.

The rest of this section provides a description of each step, while the next section details each bias, the respective metrics and mitigation actions.

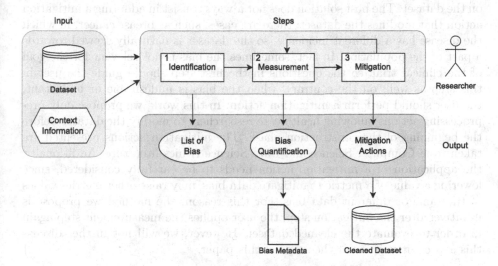

Fig. 1. The pipeline of the proposed method.

Bias Identification. This step consists in identifying data bias that may affect the dataset, and that need to be mitigated if present. Possible data bias are: minority, missing data, informativeness and selection bias. For each of them, we report the definition and a list of questions that the researcher should answer to acquire knowledge of the specific bias, in particular on the risks deriving from their presence. For this reason, the method we propose takes the form of guidelines for health care researchers to perform bias analysis on health data sources, to understand the risks connected to their usage and better know how to mitigate them.

Bias Measurement. This step consists in quantifying the identified data bias, in order to understand the magnitude of the possible impact on the results of the clinical trial. For each data bias we give an overview of the most suitable metrics, taken from the Data Science Ethics literature, to recognize and quantify it. The results of this step can be stored in metadata associated to the dataset, to be reused for future clinical trials. In fact, it is common for a dataset to be used for additional clinical trials [21,28]. Therefore, it is important to save the previously extracted information on data bias for further analyses not originally planned. To do so, our method stores information on the presence and magnitude of bias.

Bias Mitigation. The last step of the pipeline consists in choosing a mitigation action based on the previously used metric, the context and the goal of the clinical trial. The choice of the mitigation action is strictly related to the context and the goal of the trial, since each action potentially has different consequences on the dataset. The best solution does not always consist in adopting a mitigation action that modifies the dataset: there are cases, such as breast cancer, in which the disease has a different incidence, so the dataset is naturally skewed towards a part of the population. In fact, sometimes the bias is not relevant for the goal of the clinical trial, so the questions in the first step should guide the user in this step as well; on the contrary, when the bias is undesirable or important, the user should perform a mitigation action. In this work, we propose only pre-processing actions, allowing health care researchers to modify the dataset before the beginning of the construction phase. The mitigation actions presented are taken from Computer Science and Data Science Ethics literature. Additionally, the application of a mitigation action needs to be carefully considered, since lowering a value of a metric to mitigate data bias, may raise other metrics values of the same or different data bias. For this reason, the method we propose is iterative: after the mitigation step, the user applies the measurement step again in order to evaluate the cleaned dataset. However, we will not further discuss this aspect since it is not the scope of this paper.

6   Bias Identification and Measurement

This section explores the bias introduced in the previous Sect. 5, giving the definition, the measurement and the possible mitigation strategies for each one.

6.1   Minority Bias

Definition. The protected groups may have insufficient numbers of patients for a model to learn the correct statistical patterns [31, p.3].

Identification. During this step, it is important to focus on the attributes and features that are in the dataset. The following questions help health care researchers to identify this data bias.

- Which attributes and features are present in the dataset?
- Which are more relevant for the study?
- Are there protected attributes for the study? Are gender or ethnicity present in the dataset?

A group can be identified by specifying one or more characteristics of the attributes present in the dataset. Some examples of groups are: females, males,

Caucasian, Black, Asiatic, Caucasian females, Black females, etc. If at least one of these characteristics is protected, the entire group is also protected.

After answering the questions, the health care researcher starts combining the information given by the context and the goal of the clinical trial, with the identified groups. If she concludes that, given the clinical trial, the dataset is not affected by minority bias, because, for example, there is only one group, then the risks and the issues illustrated in Sect. 2 are prevented. For this reason, the identification of different groups, particularly the protected ones, is fundamental.

Measurement. To measure the number of people in the (protected) group and, consequently, the minority bias, we identify three different measurements: density, diversity and fairness. Each one studies different aspects of data representation and distribution.

First, *Density* is the degree to which different entities occur in the dataset. It is the number of occurrences of a value [27], so it represents the easiest metric to study. Figure 2 shows the density for a simple example where there are two attributes: "sex" has two values "Female" and "Male" and "ethnicity" has three values "Caucasian", "Black" and "Asiatic". It is evident from the plot that the minorities are females, Black people and Asiatic people.

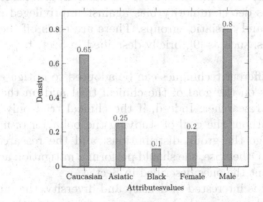

Fig. 2. Density plot

Another measurement is *diversity* that "ensures that different kinds of objects are represented in the data" [12, p.1]. The most popular metrics for diversity are based on the notions of distance or coverage [12]. A system that defines and studies coverage is given in [4], briefly described in Sect. 4. The authors developed efficient algorithms to identify uncovered regions of data. Figure 3, taken from [4], shows a sample dataset with two attributes x_1 and x_2. Every tuple in the dataset is represented by a black dot, and the uncovered region is colored in red. A green zone is a region that has a sufficient number of samples, while a red zone evidences a lack of elements and, consequently, the presence of minority bias.

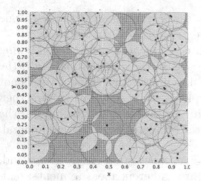

sex	
Privileged group	*Male*
Unprivileged group	*Female*
Minority bias against unprivileged group detected in	*2 out of 5 statistical metrics*
ethnicity	
Privileged group	*Caucasian*
Unprivileged groups	*Black, Asiatic*
Minority bias against unprivileged group detected in	*4 out of 5 statistical metrics*

Fig. 3. Diversity plot   **Fig. 4.** Fairness plot

To measure *fairness*, the most used metrics are statistical ones [38]: they evaluate the predictions, given by a classification model based on the dataset, compared with the actual instances of the dataset. An example of fairness analysis is given in Fig. 4. In this example we selected five statistical metrics and we analyzed the outcome of the predictions for the different groups. It is worth noticing that the metrics detect minority bias against unprivileged groups, namely "Female", "Black" and "Asiatic" groups. There are tools off-the-shelf that can provide this analysis, such as [9], briefly described in Sect. 4.

Bias Mitigation. Different techniques can be adopted to mitigate minority bias. The choice depends on the goal of the clinical trial and on the metric chosen by the health care researcher. Indeed, if the clinical trial only focuses on the majority groups, without the goal of studying the behavior of minorities, there is no need to change the group distributions, and the researcher should not modify the dataset. Otherwise, she should perform a mitigation action. For space limitation, we present the ones described in Sect. 4.

If the researcher is interested in density and diversity, the mitigation action to apply is [3], that determines the least amount of data that the researcher must add to solve the lack of representation previously discovered. If she is interested in fairness, the dataset can be modified using one of the pre-processing techniques presented in [9], such as *reweighing*, that weights the examples in each (group, label) combination differently to ensure fairness before classification, or *optimized pre-processing*, that learns a probabilistic transformation to modify the features and the labels in the data.

6.2   Missing Data Bias

Definition. Data may be missing for protected groups in a nonrandom fashion, which makes an accurate prediction hard to render [31, p.3].

Identification. "A missing value is a value that exists in the real world, but is not available in a data collection" [6, p.7]. The following questions may help health care researchers to identify this data bias.

- Are there any missing values? If so, why?

It is important to understand the reason why a value is missing. In fact, missing values are very frequent in questionnaires for medical scenarios [20]. There are three main types of missing values: *(i)* missing completely at random, i.e., the value does not depend on observed attributes or missing value, *(ii)* missing at random, i.e., it depends on observed attributes, *(iii)* missing not at random, when the value that is missing depends on the value itself [24].

To identify this data bias, the user has to concentrate on the last type of missing value. It is critical to understand the types of missing values that the dataset may have, because the user has to understand the reason why the value is missing. Unfortunately, rarely researchers can determine the type of missing value solely based on the data at hand, so context information must be considered as well [20].

Measurement. In large datasets, identifying missing values can be difficult and often requires domain knowledge. Completeness, defined as "the ratio between the number of not null values over the total number of values" [6, p.19], can be used to measure the amount of missing values. It can be computed on values, on tuple, or on attributes [7]. Given the example used for the minority bias, Table 1 shows a completeness analysis with the percentage of missing values for each attribute value.

Bias Mitigation. Three main methods can be used to mitigate the presence of missing values [19]: *(i) Deletion*, in which the researcher discards all the data with a missing values; *(ii) Single Imputation* in which the researcher converts the missing values into a new value, for example substituting the mean, the mode or other statistical values; *(iii) Model-Based*, in which the researcher assign a new value, based on a model created on the rest of the dataset. The researcher should decide the best strategy that yields the least biased estimations in the results, taking into account the context and the goal of the clinical trial. Moreover, fixing all missing values may require a considerable amount of effort. Therefore, tuples can be marked based on utility contribution, and prioritized based on the research goals. Additionally, to improve cost/effectiveness, the researcher may consider fixing only attributes that can contribute more to the prediction [6].

6.3 Informativeness Bias

Definition. Features may be less informative to render a prediction in protected groups [31, p.3].

Identification. The following questions help health care researchers to identify this data bias.

Table 1. Completeness analysis

Attribute value	% of missing values
Black	15%
Caucasian	5%
Asiatic	30%
Female	25%
Male	0%

– Which features are more important for predicting the result?
– Are there features for which more information is needed?

To understand which features are used to predict the outcome and how much they are important, the researcher has to analyze the prediction algorithm. Given an input dataset, the output of an algorithm mainly depends on the technique adopted.

Measurement. In the machine learning field, advanced techniques such as neural networks create very complex models, and the process that lead to results is not easy to understand; for this reason, they are said to be opaque. The purpose of explainability is to make explicit the interactions among the model, the learning technique adopted to produce it, and the data on which it operates; this is relevant both when we want to understand how the model works, and when we want to explain the outcome of the model for a single individual or group.

Thus, it is fundamental to study *Explainable Machine Learning*, which "highlights decision-relevant parts of the used representations of the algorithms and active parts in the algorithmic model" [17, p.3]. If we consider a prediction algorithm like logistic regression, to explain the output of the model and consequently measure this data bias, feature importance techniques can be used. In these tasks, the importance of each feature is given by the coefficient that the model associates to each feature during the training phase: these coefficients indicate how much each attribute value impacts the final output. Therefore, in order to evaluate a model with respect to the informativeness bias, it is sufficient to study and compare the feature coefficients, and to control whether the most important attributes also exhibit unfair behaviors. This way we can establish whether the learned model is informative for all groups or not.

Figure 5 shows the feature importance of the previous example: Caucasian, Male and Asiatic group have a higher probability to get a positive outcome with respect to Black and Female that, due to the negative coefficients, will probably receive a negative one.

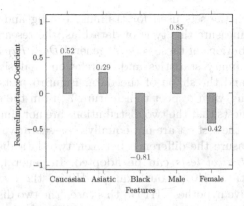

Fig. 5. Feature importance

Bias Mitigation. Given the goal and the context of the clinical trial, if all the features are informative enough, the researcher can leave the model as it is. However, as said before, not all algorithms are explainable, and feature importance is not always computable. In this case, two approaches can be adopted: *(i)* *post-hoc systems* provides local explanations for a specific decision and make it reproducible on demand, instead of explaining the whole system behavior, *(ii)* *ante-hoc systems* implements algorithms interpretable by design towards specific approaches [18], such as linear regression and decision trees. According to the context information and to the goal of the clinical trial, the researcher can adopt one of these two techniques to solve the problem of informativeness bias.

6.4   Selection Bias

Bias Definition. The training data may not be representative of the population, or the deployment data may differ from the training data. [31, p.3].

Identification. In this step, the researcher answers to the following questions.

- Are there training and testing phases for the study?
- Has the model been evaluated? If yes, how?

Given the whole available data, the procedure to construct a data analysis algorithm is the following: in a first phase, named "training phase", the model is built using a portion of the data, then in the second phase named "testing phase" the model is evaluated with the remaining data. In some cases, a part of the available data is reserved to develop the model before production: this is called "validation set" or "development set". For the researcher it is useful to understand how these sets are produced, and whether they are similar and representative of the population.

Measurement. Given the sets used for training, testing and the eventual validation, in order to measure this type of data bias, the researcher analyzes and compares the distributions of these sets. A general *Data Exploration* of the sets based on plots, summary statistics and correlation analysis is highly recommended to understand the shape of the data. Figure 6 plots the training and test sets distributions, with respect to a feature Y, from the example described above. The plot suggests that the two distributions are not similar, so in this case the training set and the test set are not equally representative of the population.

To precisely measure the difference between two data distributions and to compare them, *statistical tests* can be adopted. In general, a statistical test defines a null hypothesis H0 (in our example H0 is "the two distributions are equal"), an alternative hypothesis H1 (in this case "the two distributions are different"), and a significance level α, i.e. the probability of rejecting H0. The sampling distribution of the statistical test is computable either exactly or approximately, and the value obtained is the p-value. If the p-value is less than or equal to the chosen significance level α, then H0 is rejected in favor of H1; otherwise, if the p-value is greater than α, the null hypothesis is accepted. Usually, values of α such as 0.05 or 0.01 are chosen.

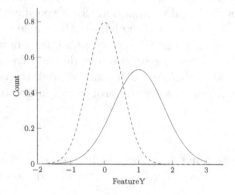

Fig. 6. Training and test sets distributions

Bias Mitigation. If the measurement step showed some inconsistencies, a mitigation procedure is needed. The split between training and test set should be performed avoiding selection bias. The most common option is to assign two third of the data for training and one third for testing. However, for small or "unbalanced" datasets, samples might not be representative. A more advanced option is to use *K-fold cross-validation* [40]: after splitting data into K subsets of equal size, each subset is used for testing one at a time, with the remaining portion of data being used for training. Standard method for evaluation is to use "repeated K-fold cross-validation", in which the K-fold cross-validation is repeated multiple times. Usually K is chosen to be 5 or 10. The special case, when $K = n$, is called "leave-one-out cross-validation", where the testing set comprises a single point and the remaining data is used for training purposes [40]. Table 2 shows a summary of all types of data bias presented with the corresponding measurement and mitigation techniques.

Table 2. Data bias summary table

Type of data bias	Measurement	Mitigation
Minority	Density	Diversity enhancement
	Diversity	
	Fairness	Reweighing
		Optimized pre-processing
Missing value	Completeness	Deletion
		Single imputation
		Model-based methods
Informativeness	Explainable ML	Ante-hoc systems
	Feature importance	Post-hoc systems
Selection	Data exploration	K-fold cross-validation
	Statistical tests	

7 Validation

A preliminary validation of our method consisted in semi-structured interviews with subjects working in the health care sector. We interviewed 5 subjects: *(i)* an oncologist and experienced health care researcher; *(ii)* a philosopher with expertise in bioethics working in a research institute; *(iii)* an experienced imaging and neuro-anatomy technician working in a research laboratory; *(iv)* a mathematician and philosopher, expert in data analysis and health care ethics; *(v)* a physician and pharmacologist working in a research institute and member of ethics committee.

In these interviews, we described our method, being as impartial as possible, and asked the following questions:

- Is the temporal placement of the method correct?
- Is the list of data bias complete?
- Is data bias correctly defined?
- Is the list of metrics complete for each data bias?
- Do the metrics correctly represent the data bias?
- Is the list of mitigation actions complete?
- Is the pipeline functional to the objectives of the method?
- Are the outputs of the method valuable for the health care researchers?

All subjects answered positively to the questions, confirming the validity of the method and underlining its importance for health care researchers and datasets. Through their answers, the subjects highlighted relevant aspects for our research such as: the seriousness of the consequences of data bias in clinical trials, the importance of contextual information and the goal in clinical trials in the application of the method, the need of a common procedure for identifying, measuring and possibly mitigating data bias. Furthermore, subjects highlighted that, for the effective usage of the method, a collaboration with a computer scientist becomes fundamental, considering that a health care researcher may not be familiar with mitigation actions. This is especially true since not all of the mitigation actions are available off-the-shelf or easily usable, due to the complexity of understanding them.

From these valuable interactions we have been able to enrich and improve our research, even correcting and adapting the method to the demands and needs of the researchers.

8   Conclusion

Clinical trials based on big data and machine learning techniques, such as data lakes and data mining, allow to analyze larger and larger datasets obtaining precise results through efficient procedures, leading to new and more reliable therapies. However, it has been shown that the complexity of their operations significantly reduces the transparency of the results obtained from their use. Therefore, it is of paramount importance to analyze and measure data bias in health care datasets, to raise the trustworthiness of clinical trials and avoid relying on erroneous results.

This paper proposes a method that guides health care researchers in achieving this objective with a pipeline that defines three steps for the identification of data bias, their measurement and mitigation. The method has been validated with semi-structured interviews that underlined the importance of the method and its outputs.

Future work will include: *(i)* further analyze the relation between data bias and mitigation actions, improving the questions provided to health care researchers; *(ii)* structure metadata for health care datasets, and integrate them in our method; *(iii)* conduct experiments on real health care datasets using our method; *(iv)* build a software tool that supports our method.

Acknowledgment. This work has been partially supported by the Health Big Data Project (CCR-2018-23669122), funded by the Italian Ministry of Economy and Finance and coordinated by the Italian Ministry of Health and the network Alleanza Contro il Cancro.

References

1. Adebayo, J.A., et al.: FairML: toolbox for diagnosing bias in predictive modeling. Ph.D. thesis, Massachusetts Institute of Technology (2016)
2. Angwin, J., Larson, J., Mattu, S., Kirchner, L.: Machine bias. In: Ethics of Data and Analytics, pp. 254–264. Auerbach Publications (2016)

3. Asudeh, A., Jin, Z., Jagadish, H.: Assessing and remedying coverage for a given dataset. In: 2019 IEEE 35th International Conference on Data Engineering, pp. 554–565. IEEE (2019)
4. Asudeh, A., Shahbazi, N., Jin, Z., Jagadish, H.: Identifying insufficient data coverage for ordinal continuous-valued attributes. In: Proceedings of International Conference on Management of Data, pp. 129–141 (2021)
5. Balayn, A., Lofi, C., Houben, G.-J.: Managing bias and unfairness in data for decision support: a survey of machine learning and data engineering approaches to identify and mitigate bias and unfairness within data management and analytics systems. VLDB J. **30**(5), 739–768 (2021). https://doi.org/10.1007/s00778-021-00671-8
6. Batini, C., Cappiello, C., Francalanci, C., Maurino, A.: Methodologies for data quality assessment and improvement. ACM Comput. Surv. **41**(3), 1–52 (2009)
7. Batini, C., Scannapieco, M.: Data and Information Quality. DSA, Springer, Cham (2016). https://doi.org/10.1007/978-3-319-24106-7
8. Beam, A.L., Kohane, I.S.: Big data and machine learning in health care. Jama **319**(13), 1317–1318 (2018)
9. Bellamy, R.K., et al.: Ai fairness 360: An extensible toolkit for detecting and mitigating algorithmic bias. IBM J. Res. Dev. **63**(4/5), 1–4 (2019)
10. Char, D.S., Shah, N.H., Magnus, D.: Implementing machine learning in health care—addressing ethical challenges. N. Engl. J. Med. **378**(11), 981 (2018)
11. Cohen, I.G., Amarasingham, R., Shah, A., Xie, B., Lo, B.: The legal and ethical concerns that arise from using complex predictive analytics in health care. Health Affairs **33**(7), 1139–1147 (2014)
12. Drosou, M., Jagadish, H.V., Pitoura, E., Stoyanovich, J.: Diversity in big data: a review. Big Data **5**(2), 73–84 (2017)
13. Esteva, A., et al.: Dermatologist-level classification of skin cancer with deep neural networks. Nature **542**(7639), 115–118 (2017)
14. Gerhard, T.: Bias: considerations for research practice. Am. J. Health Syst. Pharm. **65**(22), 2159–2168 (2008)
15. Grote, T., Berens, P.: On the ethics of algorithmic decision-making in healthcare. J. Med. Ethics **46**(3), 205–211 (2020)
16. Gulshan, V., et al.: Development and validation of a deep learning algorithm for detection of diabetic retinopathy in retinal fundus photographs. Jama **316**(22), 2402–2410 (2016)
17. Holzinger, A., Langs, G., Denk, H., Zatloukal, K., Müller, H.: Causability and explainability of artificial intelligence in medicine. Wiley Interdiscip. Rev. Data Min. Knowl. Discov. **9**(4), e1312 (2019)
18. Holzinger, A., Plass, M., Holzinger, K., Crisan, G.C., Pintea, C.M., Palade, V.: A glass-box interactive machine learning approach for solving np-hard problems with the human-in-the-loop. arXiv preprint arXiv:1708.01104 (2017)
19. Ibrahim, J.G., Chen, M.H., Lipsitz, S.R., Herring, A.H.: Missing-data methods for generalized linear models: a comparative review. J. Am. Stat. Assoc. **100**(469), 332–346 (2005)
20. Ibrahim, J.G., Chu, H., Chen, M.H.: Missing data in clinical studies: issues and methods. J. Clin. Oncol. **30**(26), 3297 (2012)
21. Knoppers, B.M.: International ethics harmonization and the global alliance for genomics and health. Genome Med. **6**(2), 1–3 (2014)
22. Krause, J., et al.: Grader variability and the importance of reference standards for evaluating machine learning models for diabetic retinopathy. Ophthalmology **125**(8), 1264–1272 (2018)

23. Lambrecht, A., Tucker, C.: Algorithmic bias? An empirical study of apparent gender-based discrimination in the display of stem career ads. Manag. Sci. **65**(7), 2966–2981 (2019)
24. Little, R.J., Rubin, D.B.: Statistical Analysis with Missing Data, vol. 793. John Wiley & Sons, Hoboken (2019)
25. Manrai, A.K., et al.: Genetic misdiagnoses and the potential for health disparities. N. Engl. J. Med. **375**(7), 655–665 (2016)
26. Mehrabi, N., Morstatter, F., Saxena, N., Lerman, K., Galstyan, A.: A survey on bias and fairness in machine learning. ACM Comput. Surv. **54**(6), 1–35 (2021)
27. Naumann, F., Freytag, J.C., Leser, U.: Completeness of integrated information sources. Inf. Syst. **29**(7), 583–615 (2004)
28. van Ommen, G.J.B., et al.: BBMRI-ERIC as a resource for pharmaceutical and life science industries: the development of biobank-based expert centres. Eur. J. Hum. Genetics **23**(7), 893–900 (2015)
29. Papakyriakopoulos, O., Mboya, A.M.: Beyond algorithmic bias: a socio-computational interrogation of the google search by image algorithm. Soc. Sci. Comput. Rev. (2021). https://doi.org/10.1177/08944393211073169
30. Pitoura, E.: Social-minded measures of data quality: fairness, diversity, and lack of bias. J. Data Inf. Qual. **12**(3), 1–8 (2020)
31. Rajkomar, A., Hardt, M., Howell, M.D., Corrado, G., Chin, M.H.: Ensuring fairness in machine learning to advance health equity. Ann. Internal Med. **169**(12), 866–872 (2018)
32. Saxena, N.A., Huang, K., DeFilippis, E., Radanovic, G., Parkes, D.C., Liu, Y.: How do fairness definitions fare? Testing public attitudes towards three algorithmic definitions of fairness in loan allocations. Artif. Intell. **283**, 103238 (2020)
33. Stoyanovich, J., Abiteboul, S., Miklau, G.: Data, responsibly: fairness, neutrality and transparency in data analysis. In: International Conference on Extending Database Technology (2016)
34. Stoyanovich, J., Howe, B.: Nutritional labels for data and models. IEEE Data Eng. Bull. **42**(3), 13–23 (2019)
35. Tillin, T., et al.: Ethnicity and prediction of cardiovascular disease: performance of qrisk2 and Framingham scores in a UK tri-ethnic prospective cohort study (sabre—southall and brent revisited). Heart **100**(1), 60–67 (2014)
36. Topol, E.J.: High-performance medicine: the convergence of human and artificial intelligence. Nat. Med. **25**(1), 44–56 (2019)
37. Tramer, F., et al.: Fairtest: discovering unwarranted associations in data-driven applications. In: IEEE European Symposium on Security and Privacy, pp. 401–416 (2017)
38. Verma, S., Rubin, J.: Fairness definitions explained. In: 2018 IEEE/ACM International Workshop on Software Fairness (fairware), pp. 1–7 (2018)
39. Wapner, J.: Cancer scientists have ignored African DNA in the search for cures. Newsweek Magazine (July 2018). https://www.newsweek.com/2018/07/27/cancer-cure-genome-cancer-treatment-africa-genetic-charles-rotimi-dna-human-1024630.html. Accessed 23 June 2022
40. Zaki, M.J., Meira Jr, W.: Data Mining and Machine Learning: Fundamental Concepts and Algorithms. Cambridge University Press, Cambridge (2020)

Clinical Synthetic Data Generation to Predict and Identify Risk Factors for Cardiovascular Diseases

Clara García-Vicente[1], David Chushig-Muzo[1],
Inmaculada Mora-Jiménez[1], Himar Fabelo[2,3], Inger Torhild Gram[4,5],
Maja-Lisa Løchen[5], Conceição Granja[4,6], and Cristina Soguero-Ruiz[1]

[1] Department of Signal Theory and Communications, Telematics and Computing
Systems, Rey Juan Carlos University, Madrid 28943, Spain
{clara.garcia.vicente,david.chushig,inmaculada.mora,
cristina.soguero}@urjc.es
[2] Research Institute for Applied Microelectronics, University of Las Palmas de Gran
Canaria, Las Palmas de Gran Canaria, Spain
hfabelo@iuma.ulpgc.es
[3] Fundación Canaria Instituto de Investigación Sanitaria de Canarias (FIISC),
Las Palmas de Gran Canaria, Spain
[4] Norwegian Centre for E-health Research, University Hospital of North Norway,
Tromsø 9019, Norway
{inger.gram,conceicao.granja}@ehealthresearch.no
[5] Faculty of Health Sciences, Department of Community Medicine,
UiT The Arctic University of Norway, Tromsø 9019, Norway
maja-lisa.lochen@uit.no
[6] Faculty of Nursing and Health Sciences, Nord University, Bodø, Norway

Abstract. Noncommunicable diseases are among the most significant
health threats in our society, being cardiovascular diseases (CVD) the most
prevalent. Because of the severity and prevalence of these illnesses, early
detection and prevention are critical for reducing the worldwide health
and economic burden. Though machine learning (ML) methods usually
outperform conventional approaches in many domains, class imbalance
can hinder the learning process. Oversampling techniques on the minority classes can help to overcome this issue. In particular, in this paper we
apply oversampling methods to categorical data, aiming to improve the
identification of risk factors associated with CVD. To conduct this study,
questionnaire data (categorical) obtained by the Norwegian Centre for E-
health Research associated with healthy and CVD patients are considered. The goal of this work is two-fold. Firstly, evaluating the influence of
combining oversampling techniques and linear/nonlinear supervised ML
methods in binary tasks. Secondly, identifying the most relevant features
for predicting healthy and CVD cases. Experimental results show that
oversampling and FS techniques help to improve CVD prediction. Specifically, the use of Generative Adversarial Networks and linear models usually
achieve the best performance (area under the curve of 67%), outperform-
ing other oversampling techniques. Synthetic data generation has proved
to be beneficial for both identifying risk factors and creating models with
reasonable generalization capability in the CVD prediction.

© The Author(s), under exclusive license to Springer Nature Switzerland AG 2022
E. K. Rezig et al. (Eds.): DMAH 2022/Poly 2022, LNCS 13814, pp. 75–91, 2022.
https://doi.org/10.1007/978-3-031-23905-2_6

Keywords: Non-communicable diseases · Cardiovascular diseases · Generative adversarial networks · SMOTE · Synthetic data generation · Feature selection · Risk factor identification

1   Introduction

Non-communicable diseases (NCDs) are among the significant health threats in our society due to their impact and severity, affecting all age ranges and countries [46]. According to the World Health Organization, NCDs are responsible for the most significant number of deaths worldwide, with approximately 41 million people dying yearly [35]. The leading NCDs are cardiovascular diseases (CVDs), cancer, chronic respiratory diseases, and diabetes mellitus, with 17.9, 9, 3.9 and 1.6 million deaths per year, respectively [18]. This accounts for 71% of all deaths globally, and although NCDs tend to be associated with old people, 15 million of these deaths occur in people within the range of 30 and 69 years. Therefore, young people, adults and the elderly may be vulnerable to risk factors related to the development of NCDs.

NCDs are caused by different factors, including genetic, physiological, behavioral and environmental factors [2]. Among them, the lack of physical activity, unhealthy diets, alcohol/tobacco use, and obesity play an important role in the onset of these diseases [36]. The main priority for NCDs prevention is linked to lifestyle change as well as early intervention. The main problem with NCDs is that they are often diagnosed at an advanced stage, making it challenging to deal with them. In this scenario, the availability of models to support decision-making would help in the early diagnosis of NCDs, as well as to identify high-risk patients and reduce mortality rates [14,30].

Over the last years, different machine learning (ML) methods have been developed to support health practitioners in decision-making, providing remarkable advances in different knowledge domains. ML techniques use data to build models capable of making predictions and identifying patterns [9]. In the clinical setting, a variety of works have applied ML in different applications, including support to disease diagnosis, extraction of hidden patterns and analysis of health statuses, among others [9]. Data availability is crucial to the success of ML classifiers which, in general, are built under the assumption of a similar number of observations per class [20]. Class imbalance usually causes that data-driven models capture a better representation of the observations in the majority class, leading to poor model performance for the minority class [45]. In real-world scenarios, when dealing with medical databases, as in our case study, the class imbalance is one of the main challenges for designing data-driven models, usually due to the limitation in the number of samples.

To cope with the class imbalance problem, a variety of methods have been proposed in the literature [21]. In this paper, we focus on oversampling techniques, with the synthetic minority oversampling technique (SMOTE) [7] being one of the most extensively used. Other approaches are increasingly coming into use, such as the Generative Adversarial Networks (GANs), which have changed findings in a variety of fields by providing high performance when generating synthetic data [1]. Although GANs have been tested in a variety of domains, they have not been thoroughly investigated when it comes to electronic health records (EHRs) [1]. In the literature, different GANs have been presented in the clinical domain to generate synthetic patient samples from real-world data, addressing the challenge of restricted data sources in healthcare applications [8]. The GAN-based model called medGAN [8] was recently presented to generate synthetic categorical data related to EHRs using the clinical code-based MIMIC dataset [28]. Most previous studies refer to the generation of synthetic data from numerical databases rather than categorical databases, even when most healthcare applications handle categorical data.

In order to achieve class balance, we created synthetic samples by focusing on the following types of data augmentation schemes: SMOTEN, a variant of SMOTE for categorical data, Tabular Variational Autoencoder (TVAE) [47], Gaussian Copula (GC) [33] and medGAN [8]. Once the classes were balanced, we applied several ML approaches to extract the most predominant risk factors and perform classification tasks. Finally, the performance of the resulting model was evaluated using a subset of real observations, independent from those considered during the model design.

The rest of the paper is organized as follows. Section 2 describes the dataset and pre-processing stage. Section 3 introduces the theoretical foundations of the oversampling and classification methods used. Next, Sect. 4 shows experimental results related to CVD classification performance and model interpretability outcomes when considering linear and nonlinear methods. Finally, Sect. 5 presents the discussion and main conclusions.

2 Dataset Description and Pre-processing

The dataset considered in this work is part of the contribution to a three-year project carried out by the Norwegian Centre for E-health Research, UiT The Arctic University of Norway and Healthcom, who designed the "Health and Disease" of NCDs [19]. A smartphone-based method was used to collect the data by a series of survey questions to a population group in Norway. This study was developed for monitoring the modifiable risk factors of four NCDs: diabetes, cancer, CVD and chronic respiratory diseases. The dataset was composed of 2303 individuals, but in the preprocessing stage we eliminated 10 individuals who had not completed the questionnaire, resulting in a dataset with a total of 2293 individuals.

The survey was designed with a total of 26 questions (variables): 7 questions related to socioeconomic factors, 7 questions related to alcohol and drug use, 4 questions related to physical activity, 7 questions related to the type of diet, and 1 question indicating current/previous NCDs. In particular, the following NCDs were considered: high cholesterol, atrial fibrillation, myocardial infarction, heart failure, stroke, chronic respiratory disease, cancer and diabetes. Finally, by studying the disease groups separately, we observed that all those who suffered or had suffered heart failure, cardiovascular accident, atrial fibrillation and/or myocardial infarction had also responded that they suffered cardiovascular disease. For this reason, we decided to group these four variables into a new variable indicating only whether the patient had CVD. Individuals who did not respond to the question related to NCDs were considered as healthy individuals. Thus, there were 465 people with CVD, 72 people with cancer, 46 people with both NCDs and 1578 people who do not suffer from any disease (associated with the healthy population group). Considering the low number of patients with cancer and both diseases, we decided to focus only on the study of CVD patients, which according to the literature it is also the predominant disease within NCDs [18]. Furthermore, we created a new category called 'NA' to indicate that the answer to a question is not available. Finally, our dataset consists of 2043 individuals, with 1578 healthy respondents and 465 individuals with CVD. Regarding the variables, we have organized them into the following six groups:

- **Socioeconomic background factors**: year of birth (age), sex, body mass index (BMI) and level of education (education).
- **Substance use**: cigarette consumption (smoking), snuff and e-cigarette use, and alcohol consumption. Concerning alcohol, there are specific variables extracted from the *Alcohol Use Disorders Identification Test* (AUDIT) [3], with information about frequency, the number of units usually consumed and the frequency of occasions of consumption of more than 6 units of alcohol.
- **Physical activity**: it was extracted from the *International Physical Activity Questionnaire* (IPAQ) [10]. There are data about: number of days of strenuous physical activity in the last 7 days, number of days of moderate physical activity in the last 7 days, number of days of walking for more than 10 min in the previous 7 days, and hours spent sitting (excluding sleeping hours) on a regular weekday in the previous 7 days.
- **Dietary intake**: servings of fruits and berries per day, lettuce and vegetable intake per day, sugary drinks and number of glasses per day, fish and number of times consumed per week, red meat and number of times consumed per week, processed meat and number of times consumed per week, and frequency with which extra salt is added to food before eating.
- **Income**: number of persons in the household over and under 18, and gross household income the previous year.
- **Clinical**: presence of high cholesterol.

Since we are dealing with categorical variables, we considered the one-hot-encoding strategy [6] for the majority of ML approaches. This type of coding creates one additional feature for each category in the variable (excepting for binary variables) and sets to '1' just the feature linked to the active category for each observation. After this encoding, the dataset dimension [23] increased to a total of 153 features.

3   Methodology for Predicting Cardiovascular Diseases

The workflow is sketched in Fig. 1. First, an exploratory analysis and preprocessing stage was performed to clean the data and ensure that the database is
curated for use by ML methods. Next, the dataset was split into two independent
sets (training and test sets), and the bootstrap resampling-based test was used
to perform FS. Subsequently, we used different oversampling methods to balance the classes and design CVD classifiers with balanced datasets. This section
describes the FS approach, the oversampling techniques and the ML methods.

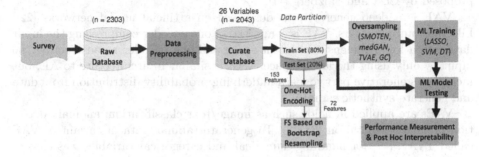

Fig. 1. Workflow using CVD data, oversampling methods and ML classifiers.

3.1   Test Based on Bootstrap Resampling for Feature Selection

High-dimensional data could lead to irrelevant and redundant features, which can
cause overfitting and worsen the model performance. To cope with these issues,
FS techniques aim to find a subset of the input variables that best describes
the underlying data structure [4]. According to the literature, FS techniques
can be categorized in filter, wrapper and embedded methods [4]. This paper
focuses on filter methods due to their simplicity and ease of implementation.
In particular, we use the non-parametric test named *bootstrap resampling* to
estimate the distribution of one statistics (*e.g.*, the mean) taking samples without
replacement from a population [16,27,31].

In our work, we compute the difference Δ between the proportion of a specific
binary feature in the CVD population and in the healthy population. To estimate
the distribution of Δ, a bootstrap resampling is performed. Thus, each class is
resampled 3,000 times, with the size of each resample being the same for both
classes. Then, the difference in proportions between the populations for each
resampling and the 95% confidence interval (CI_Δ) for each feature is computed.
The null hypothesis H_0 is true if $0 \in CI_\Delta$, while the alternative hypothesis H_1
is considered true if $0 \notin CI_\Delta$ (*e.g.*, no overlapping with 0). When H_1 is true,
it indicates a significant difference between the proportion of the same feature
in both populations (healthy and CVD individuals). Thus, features fulfilling H_1
are selected as relevant for subsequent analysis.

3.2 Oversampling Techniques for Categorical Variables

We applied the following oversampling strategies to generate synthetic samples of the minority class for categorical data:

SMOTE is one of the most popular methods for oversampling. It performs a linear interpolation of the variables associated with random samples of the minority class through the k-Nearest Neighbours scheme [17]. Since SMOTE only deals with continuous variables, variants such as SMOTEN [7,32] have been proposed for dealing with categorical variables. In SMOTEN, the nearest neighbors are found through a modified version of the value difference measure [42] proposed by Cost and Salzberg [11].

VAE is a deep generative model based on artificial neural networks [22]. Like most autoencoders, VAE is comprised of one encoder compressing the input data into a lower dimensional latent space and one decoder reconstructing the input by only using the latent space. VAE is similar in architecture to AE, but includes a generative part to learn underlying probability distribution from data and generate synthetic samples.

VAEs are applied in fields such as image/text classification, anomaly detection or image generation [38,48]. To generate tabular data, a variant of VAE called TVAE [47] for handling numerical and categorical variables was considered.

GC is a probabilistic method based on *copula functions*. A *copula* is a joint probability distribution built from marginal univariate probability distributions [33]. In other words, a copula function allows us to describe the joint probability distribution of several random variables through the dependencies among their marginal distributions.

GAN-based oversampling methods make use of neural networks. They are composed of two parts: a generative model, which we train to generate new samples, and a discriminative model which attempts to classify samples as real or synthetic (generated). Both models are trained together until the generator model produces believable examples [12]. Despite their popularity and performance, most of GAN-based methods have been used for unstructured data and in applications related to image generation. However, just a few studies have analysed GAN-based approaches for oversampling structured and tabular data. One of the most remarkable works in this line is medGAN [8], orientated to the generation of synthetic patients from EHR data.

3.3 Classification Methods

Different ML classifiers have been employed in the health-care literature [34]. To support interpretability by medical professionals as well as the identification of the most predominant risk factors for CVD, we considered the following approaches [5,26]: Least Absolute Shrinkage and Selection Operator (LASSO), Linear Support Vector Machine (LSVM), and Decision Trees (DTs).

LASSO is a technique for obtaining the best linear model for a data set by minimizing the sum of squared residuals among real and predicted values. L1 regularization is a strategy used in LASSO to penalize the previous cost function by including a term computed as the sum of the absolute values of the model coefficients [39]. As a consequence, the less relevant variables are set to zero, implicitly discarding the less relevant features in the model. The hyperparameter λ regulates the degree of penalty: the higher the λ value, the greater the penalty and the greater the number of coefficients that will be set to 0.

LSVM is a kernel-based method [29] which transforms the input space into a higher dimensional space where a hyperplane with good generalization capability is created. The main idea of SVM is to minimize the classification error by finding the maximum margin hyperplane splitting the observations into two classes. The hyperparameter C in SVM quantifies the degree of importance given to misclassifications. Different kernels have been proposed in the literature, including linear, radial basis function, sigmoid or polynomial. We used a linear kernel since its weights allows us to characterize the feature importance of the variables in an easy way [43].

DT allows to create nonlinear models in a non-parametric way. DT is composed by a set of nodes recursively divided into branches according to some criteria such as entropy [41]. When the DT just consider one feature per node, every time a node is created the associated region in the feature space is split into two parts by a linear boundary. In classification tasks, a label is assigned to each part according to the majority class among the training samples in that region. The root node (placed at the top of the tree) indicates the most relevant feature for classification, from which the first partition is performed. Below the root node are the intermediate nodes, which continue subdividing the input space. The terminal nodes indicate the final classification [41].

4 Experimental Results

This section analyzes the influence of several oversampling techniques on the classifier performance when tackling a binary classification task (healthy versus CVD individuals), and conduct a post-hoc interpretability stage.

4.1 Experimental Setup

Data-driven classifiers are designed and validated using two independent subsets, the training set and the test set, by allocating 80% and 20% of the samples, respectively. In order to better characterize the model performance, 5 independent training and test partitions have been considered in this work. For hyperparameter selection in the classifiers, the 3-fold cross validation (CV) [40] approach was considered just with the training set: λ for LASSO, C for LSVM, and both the minimum number of samples for splitting a node and the maximum tree depth for DT.

Since we are dealing with an imbalanced dataset, the area under the receiver operating characteristic (AUC) was chosen as a figure of merit for assessing the classification performance [20]. It is commonly used in the medical domain since it provides a trade-off between sensitivity and specificity. Note that, as we work with 5 partitions, the classifier performance is shown in terms of the average AUC and the standard deviation on the AUC values over the five test partitions (which remain imbalanced for evaluation purposes).

4.2   CVD Classification Performance

We present the AUC statistics when classifying healthy and CVD patients in two scenarios: (1) considering all features, and (2) only using the most relevant features according to the bootstrap resampling test. Firstly, considering only the training subset, we generate synthetic data of the minority class (CVD), aiming to balance the dataset and improve the CVD prediction. Note that for evaluating classification performance, the test subset does not present synthetic samples, and only real samples are used for getting the figures of merit. Different imbalance ratios (IRs) are considered to balance the number of samples of the dataset classes and evaluate the influence of synthetic samples on the classifier performance. IR is defined as the ratio between the number of samples of the minority class (N_{min}) and the number of samples of the majority classes (N_{maj}). Note that IR is directly related to N_{min}, with greater IR indicating more synthetic samples of the minority class (when keeping a constant value in N_{maj}) and with IR=1 indicating a balanced dataset. We compare the following oversampling techniques: SMOTEN, TVAE, GC and medGAN. We analyze the influence of N_{min} (the minority class size) in terms of AUC when varying the IR and considering different oversampling techniques (see Fig. 2 for details). Since we consider five partitions, the mean (indicated with $\circ, \triangle, \times$) and the standard deviation (represented by a shaded color) of the AUC values obtained in the test sets are shown.

We can observe in Fig. 2 that varying the IR does not substantially change the AUC values when considering TVAE, GC and SMOTEN. This means that a more significant number of synthetic samples from the minority class does not make the classification models perform better. However, in the case of medGAN, the effect of the size of the synthetic dataset (by varying IR in the interval $[0.5, 1.0]$) improves the AUC values. Secondly, medGAN seems to be the oversampling technique providing the better performance, reaching AUC $=$ 0.65 (see Fig. 2 (d)). Also, in general, we can observe that linear models (LASSO and LSVM) provide the best AUC values compared with DT. As stated, handling categorical data with one-hot encoding increases the dimensionality of the dataset considerably, with a total of $D = 153$ features. Bootstrap resampling was used to remove those features that were non-relevant and uninformative for

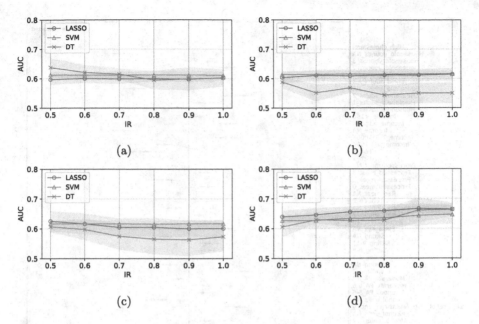

Fig. 2. Classification performance (AUC) in the test set by varying IR when considering all features and several oversampling techniques: (a) SMOTEN; (b) TVAE; (c) GC; and (d) medGAN. Solid lines refer to average AUC values, while shaded areas are associated with the corresponding standard deviation in AUC.

predicting the target variable. By applying bootstrap resampling, we take $\hat{D}$ features, being $\hat{D} < D$. With this, it is sought to evaluate if there are improvements in the classification performance and compare them.

Figures 3 and 4 show the CI_Δ for each feature when the hypothesis test based on bootstrap resampling (see Subsect. 3.1) is performed. Each CI_Δ shown in blue in Fig. 3 refers to one selected feature, with 72 out of the 153 initial features. In contrast, the CI_Δ shown in red in Fig. 4 indicates the non-selected features. It is important to highlight that features such as high cholesterol, age, BMI, household adults, house income, alcohol drink frequency, and smoking were selected. According to the literature [13,15,44], BMI, high cholesterol and age are documented as risk factors in CVD. The AUC values when considering the selected features are shown in Fig. 5. As in the previous scenario, the linear models (LASSO and LSVM) provide better AUC values than those obtained with DT.

To compare the differences in the binary classification performance using all features and the selected ones, we show in Table 1 the AUC values when considering the different test subsets (different partitions). From this table, note that the best AUC values (about 0.65 or 0.66) using all the features were obtained with medGAN. Also, focusing on this oversampling technique, the best AUC value (0.66) was achieved considering LASSO. DT presents a very similar performance, with a score of 0.66, although with a highest standard deviation (0.02

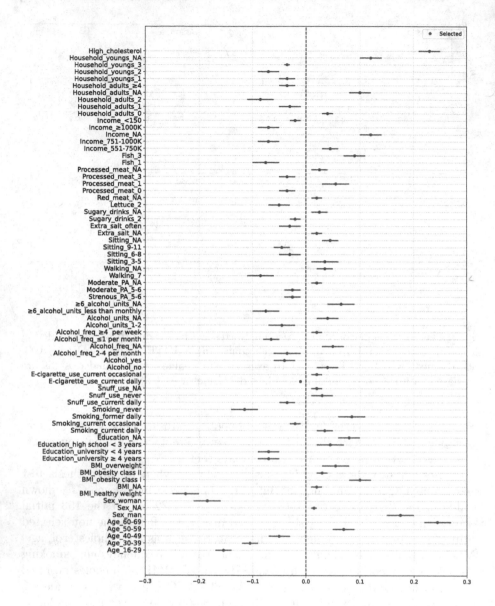

Fig. 3. CI_Δ for the selected features when considering the hypothesis test based on bootstrap resampling.

versus 0.01 of the LASSO model). From Table 1, we can conclude that better performance are obtained after FS and the best AUC values are obtained using the medGAN technique and the LASSO model.

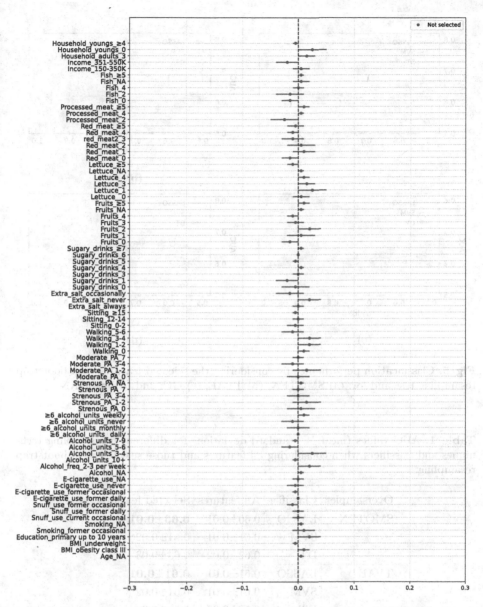

Fig. 4. CI_Δ for the non-selected features when considering the hypothesis test based on bootstrap resampling.

4.3   Post Hoc Interpretability

An important challenge in ML is the model interpretation, which refers to the reasoning behind the model decision in a way that humans can understand. In healthcare, interpretability is key to extracting knowledge and, above all, supporting physicians in decision-making. Three techniques to create interpretable

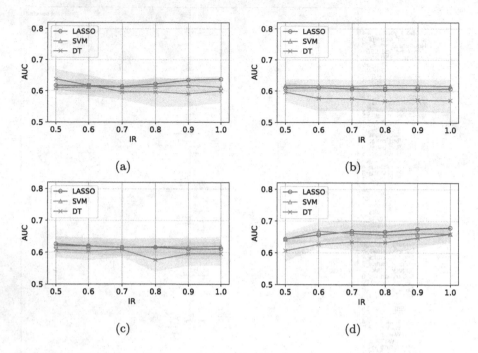

Fig. 5. Classification performance by considering the selected features with bootstrap resampling test and for: (a) SMOTEN; (b) TVAE; (c) GC; and (d) medGAN.

Table 1. AUC values (mean ± standard deviation) for different oversampling techniques and classifiers when considering all features and those selected with bootstrap resampling.

Oversampler	Classifier	All features	Selected features
SMOTEN	LASSO	0.60±0.01	**0.63±0.01**
	SVM	0.61±0.01	0.61±0.02
	DT	0.62±0.02	0.63±0.03
TVAE	LASSO	0.61±0.01	**0.61±0.01**
	SVM	0.61±0.01	0.61±0.02
	DT	0.58±0.02	0.59±0.03
GC	LASSO	0.60±0.00	**0.63±0.01**
	SVM	0.61±0.01	0.62±0.02
	DT	0.60±0.01	0.60±0.02
medGAN	LASSO	0.66±0.01	**0.67±0.01**
	SVM	0.64±0.03	0.66±0.03
	DT	0.66±0.02	0.65±0.02

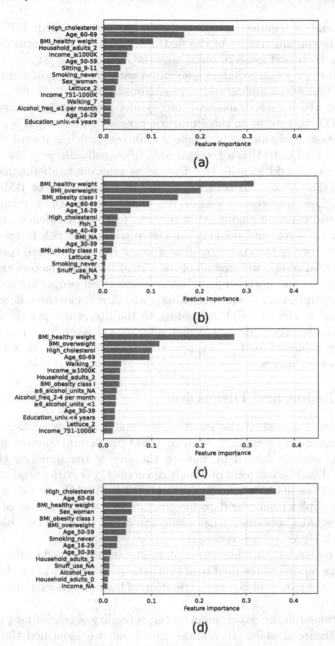

Fig. 6. Feature importance provided by DT when considering: (a) SMOTEN; (b) TVAE; (c) GC; and (d) medGAN. Note that features in each panel are sorted according to their feature importance value.

models (see Sect. 3.3) were used in this work. On the one hand, two linear models (LASSO and SVM) were analyzed since the coefficient weighting each feature provides us with information on their relevance in the class prediction [29]. On the other hand, a nonlinear classifier (DT) has been studied. DTs also allow us to identify the importance of the features, assigning a score to each feature according to their usefulness in predicting the output class [24].

The feature importance values associated with DT are shown in Fig. 6 when considering four oversampling techniques. Note that age, BMI, high cholesterol (by denoting the presence/absence) and gender were the more representative features in DT. According to the literature, excessive adiposity is a major cause of hypertension, dyslipidemia and type 2 diabetes, which is one of the primary precursors of CVDs. BMI is a key indicator of overall adiposity [44]. Our data-driven approach could identify this feature as relevant to distinguishing CVD cases. Note that in all panels of Fig. 6, the features linked to BMI are those with the highest importance values. We highlighted features related to high cholesterol and smoking among other relevant features. Evidence suggests that high cholesterol levels and smoking are two predominant risk factors for CVD, which are also two of the leading causes of death in industrialized countries [13]. The literature also supports that all of these modifiable risk factors are prevalent in all age groups and both genders, but increase when people get older [15,25]. Another relevant aspect is that individuals with low socioeconomic status seem to have a higher risk of CVD. According to the literature, people with higher socioeconomic backgrounds and higher educational level have more access to nutritionally balanced food [37], supporting that diet is considered one of the most crucial risk factors.

5   Conclusion and Discussion

In this paper, we studied the effectiveness and feasibility of using oversampling techniques on categorical data for CVD prediction. Several state-of-the-art methods were evaluated by varying the size of the minority class subset in a binary classification scenario (healthy versus CVD patients). Experimental results showed medGAN outperformed SMOTEN, TVAE and GC when generating new samples from real data in our dataset. Also in favour of medGAN, note that the AUC obtained when using the other three oversamplers did not improve with IR as N_{maj} is constant.

Further research in this line may explore a quantitative and qualitative framework analysis related to the quality of synthetic data, measuring and comparing, for instance, the joint probability distribution of features associated with real and synthetic data.

As mentioned in the paper, model interpretability is crucial for practitioners in the healthcare domain. To address this issue, we identified the most representative features for both linear (LASSO and LSVM) and nonlinear classifiers (DT). According to the coefficient values and the feature importance indexes, the most relevant risk factors associated with CVD were age, BMI, high cholesterol, gender and smoking. These findings are in line with the state-of-the-art [13,15,25,44,49].

Our work reveals that the combination of medGAN and LASSO achieve the best classification performance, reaching an average AUC value of about 67.90%.

Furthermore, using an FS technique allows us to improve the CVD prediction, obtaining higher AUC values and identifying the most representative features for CVD. In summary, the results in this study show that the combination of FS and oversampling strategies improve the prediction efficiency of healthy and CVD cases, allowing their extrapolation to more complex scenarios.

Acknowledgements. This work has been partly supported by European Commission through the H2020-EU.3.1.4.2., European Project WARIFA (Watching the risk factors: Artificial intelligence and the prevention of chronic conditions) under Grant Agreement 101017385; and by the Spanish Government by the Spanish Grants BigTheory (PID2019-106623RB-C41), and AAVis-BMR PID2019-107768RA-I00); Project Ref. 2020-661, financed by Rey Juan Carlos University and Community of Madrid; and by the Research Council of Norway (HELSE-EU-project 269882).

References

1. Aggarwal, A., et al.: Generative adversarial network: an overview of theory and applications. Int. J. Inf. Manag. Data Insights **1**(1), 100004 (2021)
2. Budreviciute, A., et al.: Management and prevention strategies for non-communicable diseases (ncds) and their risk factors. Front. Public Health **8**, 788 (2020)
3. Bush, K., et al.: The audit alcohol consumption questions (audit-c): an effective brief screening test for problem drinking. Arch. Internal Med. **158**(16), 1789–1795 (1998)
4. Cai, J., et al.: Feature selection in machine learning: a new perspective. Neurocomputing **300**, 70–79 (2018)
5. Carvalho, D.V., et al.: Machine learning interpretability: a survey on methods and metrics. Electronics **8**(8), 832 (2019)
6. Cerda, P., et al.: Similarity encoding for learning with dirty categorical variables. Mach. Learn. **107**(8), 1477–1494 (2018)
7. Chawla, N.V., et al.: Smote: synthetic minority over-sampling technique. J. Artif. Intell. Res. **16**, 321–357 (2002)
8. Choi, E., et al.: Generating multi-label discrete patient records using generative adversarial networks. In: Machine Learning for Healthcare Conference, pp. 286–305. PMLR (2017)
9. Chushig-Muzo, D., et al.: Interpreting clinical latent representations using autoencoders and probabilistic models. Artif. Intell. Med. **122**, 102211 (2021)
10. Cleland, C., et al.: Validity of the international physical activity questionnaire (ipaq) for assessing moderate-to-vigorous physical activity and sedentary behaviour of older adults in the united kingdom. BMC Med. Res. Methodol. **18**(1), 1–12 (2018)
11. Cost, S., Salzberg, S.: A weighted nearest neighbor algorithm for learning with symbolic features. Mach. Learn. **10**(1), 57–78 (1993)
12. Creswell, A., White, T., Dumoulin, V., Arulkumaran, K., Sengupta, B., Bharath, A.A.: Generative adversarial networks: an overview. IEEE Signal Process. Maga. **35**(1), 53–65 (2018)
13. Dahlöf, B.: Cardiovascular disease risk factors: epidemiology and risk assessment. Am. J. Cardiol. **105**(1), 3A-9A (2010)

14. Davagdorj, K., et al.: Explainable artificial intelligence based framework for non-communicable diseases prediction. IEEE Access **9**, 123672–123688 (2021)
15. Díez, J.M.B., et al.: Cardiovascular disease epidemiology and risk factors in primary care. Revista Española de Cardiología (English Edition) **58**(4), 367–373 (2005)
16. Efron, B., Tibshirani, R.J.: An Introduction to the Bootstrap. CRC Press, Boca Raton (1994)
17. Fernández, A., et al.: Smote for learning from imbalanced data: progress and challenges. Mark. 15-year Anni. **61**, 863–905 (2018)
18. Forouzanfar, M.H., et al.: Global, regional, and national comparative risk assessment of 79 behavioural, environmental and occupational, and metabolic risks or clusters of risks, 1990–2015: a systematic analysis for the global burden of disease study 2015. The Lancet **388**(10053), 1659–1724 (2016)
19. Gram, I.T., et al.: A smartphone-based information communication technology solution for primary modifiable risk factors for noncommunicable diseases: Pilot and feasibility study in norway. JMIR Format. Res. **6**(2), e33636 (2022)
20. He, H., Garcia, E.A.: Learning from imbalanced data. IEEE Trans. Knowl. Data Eng. **21**(9), 1263–1284 (2009)
21. Japkowicz, N., et al.: Learning from imbalanced data sets: a comparison of various strategies. In: AAAI Workshop on Learning from Imbalanced Data Sets, vol. 68, pp. 10–15. AAAI Press Menlo Park, CA (2000)
22. Kingma, D.P., Welling, M.: Auto-encoding variational bayes. arXiv preprint arXiv:1312.6114 (2013)
23. Kunanbayev, K., et al.: Complex encoding. In: International Joint Conference on Neural Networks, pp. 1–6. IEEE (2021)
24. Lavanya, D., Rani, K.U.: Performance evaluation of decision tree classifiers on medical datasets. Int. J. Comput. Appl. **26**(4), 1–4 (2011)
25. Maas, A.H., Appelman, Y.E.: Gender differences in coronary heart disease. Netherlands Heart J. **18**(12), 598–603 (2010)
26. Marchese Robinson, R.L., et al.: Comparison of the predictive performance and interpretability of random forest and linear models on benchmark data sets. J. Chem. Inf. Model. **57**(8), 1773–1792 (2017)
27. Martínez-Agüero, S., et al.: Interpretable clinical time-series modeling with intelligent feature selection for early prediction of antimicrobial multidrug resistance. Future Gener. Comput. Syst. **133**, 68–83 (2022)
28. Meng, C., et al.: Interpretability and fairness evaluation of deep learning models on mimic-iv dataset. Sci. Rep. **12**(1), 1–28 (2022)
29. Meyer, D., Wien, F.T.: Support vector machines. The Interface to libsvm in Package e1071 28 (2015)
30. Mohd Noor, N.A., et al.: Consumer attitudes toward dietary supplements consumption. Int. J. Pharm. Healthcare Mark. **8**(1), 6–26 (2014)
31. Mora-Jiménez, I., et al.: Artificial intelligence to get insights of multi-drug resistance risk factors during the first 48 hours from icu admission. Antibiotics **10**(3), 239 (2021)
32. Naim, F.A., Hannan, U.H., Humayun Kabir, M.: Effective rate of minority class over-sampling for maximizing the imbalanced dataset model performance. In: Gupta, D., Polkowski, Z., Khanna, A., Bhattacharyya, S., Castillo, O. (eds.) Proceedings of Data Analytics and Management. LNDECT, vol. 91, pp. 9–20. Springer, Singapore (2022). https://doi.org/10.1007/978-981-16-6285-0_2
33. Nelsen, R.B.: An Introduction to Copulas. Springer, Heidelberg (2007). https://doi.org/10.1007/0-387-28678-0

34. Ngiam, K.Y., Khor, W.: Big data and machine learning algorithms for health-care delivery. Lancet Oncol. **20**(5), e262–e273 (2019)
35. Organization, W.H., et al.: Noncommunicable diseases country profiles 2018 (2018)
36. Organization, W.H., et al.: Noncommunicable diseases: progress monitor 2020 (2020)
37. Psaltopoulou, T., Hatzis, G., et al.: Socioeconomic status and risk factors for cardiovascular disease: impact of dietary mediators. Hellenic J. Cardiol. **58**(1), 32–42 (2017)
38. Pu, Y., et al.: Variational autoencoder for deep learning of images, labels and captions. Adv. Neural Inf. Process. Syst. **29**(1), 295–308 (2019)
39. Ranstam, J., Cook, J.: Lasso regression. J. Brit. Surg. **105**(10), 1348–1348 (2018)
40. Refaeilzadeh, P., et al.: Cross-validation. Encycl. Database Syst. **5**, 532–538 (2009)
41. Safavian, S.R., Landgrebe, D.: A survey of decision tree classifier methodology. IEEE Trans. Syst. Man Cybern. **21**(3), 660–674 (1991)
42. Stanfill, C., Waltz, D.: Toward memory-based reasoning. Commun. ACM **29**(12), 1213–1228 (1986)
43. Steinwart, I., Christmann, A.: Support Vector Machines. Springer, Heidelberg (2008). https://doi.org/10.1007/978-0-387-77242-4
44. Taylor, H.A., Jr., et al.: Relationships of bmi to cardiovascular risk factors differ by ethnicity. Obesity **18**(8), 1638–1645 (2010)
45. Van Rijsbergen, C.J.: The Geometry of Information Retrieval. Cambridge University Press, Cambridge (2004)
46. Wagner, K.H., Brath, H.: A global view on the development of non communicable diseases. Prev. Med. **54**, S38–S41 (2012)
47. Xu, L., et al.: Modeling tabular data using conditional gan. Adv. Neural Inf. Process. Syst. **32** (2019)
48. Xu, W., Tan, Y.: Semisupervised text classification by variational autoencoder. IEEE Trans. Neural Netw. Learn. Syst. **31**(1), 295–308 (2019)
49. Yusuf, H.R., et al.: Impact of multiple risk factor profiles on determining cardiovascular disease risk. Prev. Med. **27**(1), 1–9 (1998)

Author Index

Printed in the United States
by Baker & Taylor Publisher Services